Cravings, Lies & Dopamine

Interrupting the Thought Spiral and Reclaiming Your Power

Built from the Inside: Used to Survive Series

Book 4

Cravings, Lies & Dopamine
Interrupting the Thought Spiral and Reclaiming Your Power
Copyright © 2025 BuildingBlocs Literacy LLC
All Rights Reserved

For licensing, training, or implementation inquiries, contact the publisher:

BuildingBlocs Literacy LLC
Attn: Aaron B. Kershaw
Hillside Lake
Wappingers Falls, NY 12590
(845) 600-9767
www.BuildingBlocs.org

www.TheBrightPathAcademy.com

Licensing & Usage Disclaimer

This manual is the intellectual property of BuildingBlocs Literacy LLC and is protected under U.S. and international copyright law.

This publication is meant as a source of valuable information for participants. It is not meant as a substitute for direct expert assistance. Contact a licensed professional if you require help with a diagnosis, intervention, treatment, or have symptoms such as depression, post-traumatic stress disorder (PTSD), or substance abuse. If you or someone you know is contemplating suicide, seek emergency services immediately.

Although the author(s) have made every effort to ensure the information in this book was correct at press time, the author does not assume and hereby disclaims liability for errors or omissions, whether such errors or omissions resulted from negligence, accident, or any other cause.

Unauthorized Use Prohibited

The systems described herein including but not limited to:

- Tiered certification tracks (T1–T6)
- Check-In, Reset, Red Flag™ tools
- Mentor/facilitator/director role structures
- Certification rubrics, pacing models, and LMS structures
- Participant workbooks, coaching guides, or fidelity tools

...are the **protected operational property** of BuildingBlocs Literacy LLC and the BRIGHTPath™ Academy.

Reproduction, facilitation, training delivery, implementation, or public sharing of this system or its components, whether partial or in full, without a licensing agreement is strictly prohibited.

Implementation Requires Licensing

To implement, train with, or distribute any portion of the Built from the Inside™ or Pathlight™, or *Used to Survive*™ systems, you must first obtain:

- An **active licensing agreement**
- Access to the BRIGHTPath™ LMS and certification tools
- Official training and approval by BuildingBlocs Literacy LLC or its licensed agents

For licensing inquiries, program demos, or partnership requests, please contact:

info@TheBrightPathAcademy.com
www.TheBrightPathAcademy.com
www.BuildingBlocs.org

Foreword

By Brian Wall, LPC-S,

If there is one stage of recovery that exposes the fragile line between progress and relapse, it is cravings. Not the cravings people expect; the "I need a hit right now" intensity, but the subtle, relentless whispers. The thought spirals. The mental negotiations that convince a person they can handle "just one." In my decades of work with men in behavioral health and corrections, I have seen more people undone by the quiet persistence of cravings than by the dramatic storms.

That's why Cravings, Lies & Dopamine is such a vital part of the Used to Survive series. Most resources address cravings with simple slogans: "just say no," "ride it out," or "distract yourself." But those surface-level strategies rarely hold up in the heat of the moment. What Aaron Kershaw has done in this book is cut deeper, naming the lies cravings whisper, explaining the brain science behind them, and then offering tools to interrupt the spiral before it becomes a relapse.

When I first read this volume, I was struck by how accurate and unflinching it was. Cravings aren't just about desire for the drug. They are about longing for relief, escape, control, and familiarity. They are about the nervous system chasing a dopamine spike it has been conditioned to expect. And they are about the shame that follows when those thoughts surface, leaving people convinced they are broken because they still want something they know has hurt them.

This book dismantles that shame by reframing cravings as normal, not as a moral failure, but as a predictable neurological and emotional response. That shift is powerful. When participants understand that cravings are not proof of weakness but evidence of a brain and body recalibrating, they stop wasting energy on self-hatred and can instead focus on strategy.

What makes this book practical is the toolbox it provides. The tools are tangible, repeatable practices that anyone can use in the moment. In my own professional setting, I've seen participants regain confidence when they realize they can predict cravings, label them, and ride them out without collapsing. That confidence is often what keeps them moving forward instead of giving in.

For facilitators and clinicians, this book is equally valuable. It provides a language for discussing cravings without shame, a framework for guiding clients through thought spirals, and a set of strategies that align with both trauma-informed practice and evidence-based

neuroscience. It allows professionals to validate the struggle while equipping clients with tools to win the moment.

For every person who has ever thought, "If I still crave it, I must be failing," this book is a revelation. Cravings don't mean failure. They mean you're human, you're healing, and you're ready to learn a new way to stand in your power. That is the message of this book, and it is one I fully endorse.

Brian Wall, LPC-S, LAC
Division Director, Men's Residential Behavioral Health Services
South Carolina Department of Corrections

Table of Contents

Introduction: Cravings, Lies & Dopamine

This is **Book 4 in the *Used to Survive* series**, but whether this is the first one you're picking up or you've walked with me from the beginning, you're in the right place. Every book in this series is written so it can stand on its own, because recovery is not a neat staircase. It doesn't move in clean stages, one after another. It zigzags. It doubles back. It hits you sideways when you thought you were steady.

So if you landed here first, welcome. If you've already read the earlier books, you know how this fits into the bigger picture. Either way, you're not behind and you're not lost. You're exactly where you need to be.

Let's set the frame.

- **Book 1: Why You Used** was about looking back. It broke open the truth that you didn't use because you were weak or worthless. You used because substances became survival. They numbed the pain, masked the chaos, and gave your nervous system a way to keep going when nothing else worked. It named the root.

- **Book 2: Building Life After the Burn** took on what happens after the fire. Sobriety doesn't give you your old life back, it strips it away. That book was about rebuilding identity, trust, and relationships when the scaffolding of substances is gone.

- **Book 3: Clean Enough** went deep into the "gray zone." The flatness. The hollow mornings. The sense that recovery is supposed to feel good but instead feels joyless, restless, or numb. That book helped you understand that emptiness isn't failure, it's recalibration. Healing at the speed of nerve cells.

Now comes **Book 4: Cravings, Lies & Dopamine.**

Here's why this book matters: **because cravings don't go away just because you've put down the substance.** They may hit in week one, month six, year two, or after a decade clean. They come dressed as thoughts, as body pulls, as whispers that start small but build into storms if you don't recognize them.

And cravings are sneaky. They don't just say, *"Use again."* They come wrapped in lies:

- *"It's just once."*

- *"I can handle it now."*

- *"Nobody will know."*

- *"This isn't really relapse, it's relief."*

This book dismantles those lies. It pulls cravings out of the shadows and puts them under a spotlight so they lose their power.

Here's what you'll learn as you move through these chapters:

- What cravings really are: not proof of failure, but proof your brain remembers. They're dopamine waves, not destiny.

- How the *craving loop* works, emotion → thought → justification → action → shame → repeat, and how to break it before it breaks you.

- The role of anxiety, shame, and loneliness in triggering urges, and how to interrupt those setups before they spin out.

- How to build a *craving kit* you can actually use, real tools for real moments, not just slogans.

- How to surf an urge instead of drowning in it, using body-based resets and the 90-second window of craving science.

- Why dopamine isn't your enemy, and how to rebuild healthy pleasure pathways so your brain stops screaming for the old fix.

- And most importantly: how to accept cravings as part of recovery without letting them run your life.

As always, you won't just hear from me. You'll see the clinical and body-based lenses too:

- **Nurse C** will break down what's happening in your nervous system when cravings hit, and why your body reacts like it's life-or-death.

- **Dr. Jones** will unpack the trauma side, how shame, avoidance, and unresolved grief make cravings louder, and what it takes to step out of that spiral.

Each chapter comes with tools you can use right away: trackers, checklists, reflection prompts, and recovery practices you can make your own. Nothing here is theory for theory's sake, it's all written so you can pick it up, use it in the middle of an urge, and keep moving forward.

If you only read this book, you'll leave with a set of strategies that can keep you standing when cravings come. If you walk through the whole *Used to Survive* series, you'll see how all the pieces connect: the reasons you used, the rebuilding after the burn, the gray zone of early recovery, and now cravings, the constant background noise that tries to pull you back.

But here's the bottom line: **a craving is not a command.**

It's a signal. A memory. A wave. And like every wave, it rises, it peaks, and it passes.

This book is about making sure that when it passes, you're still standing.

Because "clean enough" doesn't mean perfect. It means you're alive. And alive is enough.

How to Use This Series in Structured Recovery Programming

A Weekly Curriculum Framework for Individual and Group Work

The *Used to Survive* series was developed not only as a reading tool, but as a **modular, week-by-week recovery curriculum** that integrates with existing outpatient, residential, or community-based treatment structures.

Each book in the series aligns with one core theme of addiction recovery, from trauma and triggers to cravings, shame, and emotional regulation. The content is divided into 10 core chapters, each designed to support:

- Weekly **individual therapy sessions** (with focused prompts, narrative grounding, and emotional insight)

- Weekly **group facilitation** (using shared language, tools, and lived experience for peer connection)

- Weekly **self-directed reading** (with accessible science, real-life strategies, and body-mind integration)

Curriculum Structure Per Book

Each *Used to Survive* title can be delivered across a 10-week cycle:

Week	Chapter Theme	Individual Focus	Group Focus
1	Nervous System & Anxiety	Mapping internal "threat" systems	Shared language around feeling "on edge"
2	Attention & Impulsivity	Executive function support	Discussing shame around "chaos"
3	Loneliness & Neglect	Attachment wounds	Peer connection and rejection sensitivity
4	Trauma Triggers	Flashback and dissociation mapping	Sharing "body memories" and reactivity
5	Cravings & Dopamine	Identifying personal habit loops	Breaking cycles together
6	Food/Sleep/Mood	HALT application and physical resets	Building sustainable structure
7	Shame & Identity	"Bad person" narratives	External vs. internal stigma dialogue
8	Dissociation & Avoidance	Rest vs. numbing	Gentle reintegration practices
9	Addiction as Survival	Grief of what addiction *gave*	Collective identity reconstruction
10	Building Pause & Power	Urge surfing + emotional tools	Emergency toolkit sharing & closure

Included in Each Chapter

- Real-life narrative (Uncle Aaron)

- Physical health anchor (Nurse C)

- Clinical advisory (Dr. Jones, when applicable)

- Visual tools (fillables, tracking sheets, grounding cues)

- Three-pronged exercises:

  - Immediate Action
  - Integration Practice
  - Long-Term Anchor

- Reflection prompts for journal or session use

For Clinicians and Facilitators

This series supports trauma-informed practice through:

- Co-regulation strategies

- Cultural humility and lived experience integration

- Autonomy-supportive structure (no forced disclosure)

- Harm reduction alignment

- CASEL and SEL benchmarks for identity, emotion regulation, and decision-making

Facilitators are encouraged to use the books **in any order**, depending on client need. The first book, *Why You Used*, is foundational and recommended for opening, especially for individuals who have struggled to connect with other treatment models.

Chapter 1 – The Craving Isn't the Problem

This Chapter Will Cover:

- Why cravings are signals, not moral failures.

- How dopamine waves create the "urge curve", and why cravings peak and fall within 90 seconds.

- How to separate craving from action, recognizing the difference between information and destiny.

- The shame trap: why people confuse craving with relapse.

CASEL Alignment

- **Self-Awareness:** Naming cravings as brain-body signals, not evidence of weakness or relapse.

- **Self-Management:** Using structured tools (90-Second Reset, EMO-PATH™ Core 7) to tolerate urges without collapse.

- **Responsible Decision-Making:** Learning that a craving does not dictate behavior; practicing separation between impulse and action.

Cravings Aren't Failure

Let's set the record straight. **Having a craving does not mean you're failing.** It doesn't mean recovery isn't working. It doesn't mean relapse is inevitable.

A craving is your brain's way of saying: *"Hey, this is how we used to handle discomfort. Do you want to do that again?"* It's a learned signal. A loop firing. Nothing more.

Think of it like an old ringtone. Even years after you've switched phones, if you hear that sound in a store, your head will whip around. Not because you still own that phone, but because your brain remembers. That's how cravings work. They're echoes of a past solution, not proof that you're broken in the present.

The problem is, most people don't know this. They feel a craving rise in their chest, that quick flash of memory, that body-ache pull, and panic: *"Oh no, I must be backsliding."* Shame jumps in fast, whispering: *"If you wanted it, you must still be that person. You'll never change."*

That's not science. That's stigma.

The science is this: **cravings are dopamine waves.** Dopamine is not the "pleasure chemical" like headlines claim. It's the motivation signal. It pushes you toward seeking. In addiction, dopamine circuits get hijacked, rewired to believe the substance is the fastest, only, or best way to soothe pain. That wiring doesn't vanish just because you quit. It lingers like muscle memory.

And here's the good news: cravings follow a predictable curve. They rise, peak, and fade, usually in about 90 seconds. That's the urge curve. If you can ride the wave, you will come down the other side without acting on it.

Plain language: *A craving is a wave, not a command. It's a thought, not a verdict. It's a memory, not a destiny.*

When you understand that, you stop panicking at the first sign of craving. You stop confusing signal with relapse. And you start building power in the pause between the urge and your choice.

Why the Brain Feeds You Lies

Here's the sneaky part: cravings rarely show up naked. They don't just whisper *"use."* They dress up in lies:

- *"It's just once."*

- *"I can handle it now."*

- *"Nobody will know."*

- *"I deserve a break."*

- *"This time will be different."*

These lies don't come from nowhere. They're the brain's attempt to justify the urge. Craving itself is uncomfortable, it feels like restlessness in your skin, pressure in your chest, buzzing under your skin. The brain hates discomfort. So it starts spinning stories that would make the discomfort go away fast.

If you've ever argued with yourself during a craving, you know what I mean. One part of you is screaming *"I need it."* Another part is whispering *"Don't do it."* And you bounce back and forth until either the craving passes or you give in.

The trap is thinking the craving means you've already failed. That shame-laced thought, *"If I want it, I'm weak"*, is what makes relapse more likely, not the craving itself.

Imagine a smoke alarm going off in your house. It doesn't mean the house is on fire. It means the alarm was triggered. Maybe it's smoke from cooking. Maybe it's dust. Maybe it's an actual fire. But the alarm itself isn't the danger, it's the signal.

Cravings are the same. They're alarms. They can tell you: *"I'm stressed," "I'm lonely," "I'm bored," "I'm ashamed," "I'm hungry,"* or *"I'm tired."* The substance was once the solution to all those states. Now it's not. But the signal still fires.

That's why cravings are information, not destiny. They're your brain's way of saying: *"Something needs tending."*

The work of this chapter is to learn how to listen without obeying.

Riding the Wave: The 90-Second Reset

This is where science becomes survival. The 90-second reset is a simple, powerful tool for handling cravings in real time. Here's how it works:

Step 1: Name It.
When the craving hits, say it out loud or write it down: *"I'm craving right now."* Naming it pulls it out of the shadows and reduces shame.

Step 2: Ground the Body.
Plant your feet. Breathe deep into your belly. Pick up something cold, splash water on your face, or squeeze your hands together. These physical actions interrupt the automatic spiral.

Step 3: Wait 90 Seconds.
Set a timer if you need to. Cravings follow a curve. They rise, peak, and fall. If you can stay with yourself for that window, you'll feel it pass.

Step 4: Redirect the Energy.
Once the peak is over, shift into another action: walk, call someone, journal, stretch, drink water. Anything that moves the body and mind forward without substance.

Plain language: *Cravings are waves. The 90-second reset is your surfboard. It doesn't stop the wave, but it keeps you from drowning.*

The more you practice, the more confidence you build: *"I can feel this and not act on it."* That's recovery power.

The Takeaway

Cravings don't mean you're broken. They don't mean relapse is inevitable. They're echoes of an old system, alarms without a fire, memories that your body still rehearses. When you treat them as verdicts, shame takes over and drives you closer to using. When you treat them as signals, you get the chance to respond differently.

The wave always rises, peaks, and falls. You can ride it. Naming the craving, grounding your body, and waiting out the curve turns panic into proof: *I can feel this and stay standing.*

Plain language: cravings aren't failure. They're feedback. And every time you survive one, you teach your brain a new truth, I don't have to obey this anymore.

The First Panic

Leah was 23, six weeks clean, when it happened. She was walking past a corner store when the craving hit her chest like a punch. Her palms went sweaty. Her thoughts raced: *"Oh God, I want it. I must be failing. This means I'm going to relapse."*

By the time she got home, she was shaking. She called her sponsor in tears: *"I thought I was doing so good, but I wanted it today. I must be broken."*

Her sponsor laughed gently. *"You're not broken. You're human. Cravings happen. That wasn't relapse. That was your brain remembering. And the fact you called me instead of using? That's recovery."*

Leah's panic was common: she thought craving = relapse. Once she learned about the urge curve, she realized that her craving lasted less than two minutes. It came, peaked, passed. And she was still clean.

That shift, from shame to understanding, changed her relationship to cravings. They stopped being monsters in the dark. They became signals she could ride through.

Tools & Exercises

Immediate Action: 90-Second Reset

Purpose: To survive cravings without collapse.

How to Do It:

1. **Name the craving aloud.**
   Say: "This is a craving. Not a command." Naming it breaks the trance.

2. **Anchor your body.**
   Try a cold splash of water, deep exhale, or tense-and-release of fists and jaw.

3. **Set a timer for 90 seconds.**
   Sit still. Let the craving rise. Don't fix it. Just feel it.

4. **Redirect into a neutral action.**
   Walk the hallway. Stretch your hands. Doodle. Move without meaning.

Why It Works:
Cravings peak and fall in 90-second waves. If you survive the first hit, you gain the ground.

Integration Practice: EMO-PATH™ Core 7 Craving Map

Purpose: To uncover what your cravings are *actually* trying to tell you.

How to Do It:
When a craving hits, fill out the Core 7 framework:

- **Event:** What triggered it?

- **Mood:** Name the feeling.

- **Thought:** What lie did the craving whisper?

- **Body Sensation:** Where did you feel it (tight chest, buzzing skin, clenched jaw)?

- **Impulse:** What did you want to do?

- **Protective Action:** What did you actually do instead?

- **Hopeful Anchor:** What truth are you holding onto now?

Weekly Review Tip:
Look for trends. Do cravings show up more when you're tired, bored, lonely, or after a specific person or place?

The craving isn't the real problem. It's the lie wrapped around the craving. This map helps you untangle it.

Long-Term Anchor: Craving Log

Purpose: To track cravings over time and measure your emotional endurance.

How to Do It:

1. Use a blank calendar or notebook. Each day, mark:

   o Did you have a craving? (✔ or ✘)

   o Intensity from 1 (mild) to 10 (panic).

   o One thing you did instead of using.

2. At the end of 30 days, ask:

   o Did the cravings shrink?

   o Did your actions get stronger?

   o Did you interrupt any patterns?

Why It Works:
This is your **evidence file.** It shows you're not stuck, you're progressing. Even if it's messy.

Exercises

Craving Lie Loop Tracker

Purpose: To interrupt the lie-based thinking before action.
How to Do It:

1. Draw the cycle: **Emotion → Thought → Justification → Action → Shame**

2. Each time you feel a craving, write one line in each step.

3. Name the lie: What thought tried to justify the craving?

4. Circle where you could have interrupted the loop.

Why It Works: Naming the lie gives you back your power.

Narration Script Practice

Purpose: To give yourself a script *before* the craving hits.
How to Do It:

1. Write out a short script you can say when a craving appears.
   Example: *"This is a craving. It's not who I am. I've survived worse. I can wait 90 seconds."*

2. Practice saying it daily, even when you're calm.

3. Record yourself. Play it when you're overwhelmed.

Why It Works: Rehearsing your voice during peace makes it easier to trust during panic.

Craving State Map

Purpose: To build craving awareness through color-coding.
How to Do It:

1. At the end of each day, ask:

   - Did I have a craving today?

   - Was it **Green** (mild), **Yellow** (moderate), or **Red** (urgent)?

   - How did I respond?

2. Keep a visual tracker. Over time, notice if your Red days become Yellow, and Yellow become Green.

Why It Works: You can't fight what you don't notice. Color tracking brings visibility and agency.

Dr. Jones' Advisory	Nurse C's Note
Trauma survivors often mistake craving for relapse because both are wrapped in shame. The body remembers, and when that memory surfaces, it feels like failure. Clinically, we frame cravings as conditioned responses, like a soldier ducking at fireworks. It doesn't mean the war is still happening. It means the body remembers. Therapy helps uncouple the memory from the mandate. Cravings can be felt, named, and tolerated without action. That's resilience.	Cravings are not weakness; they are neurological echoes. Your dopamine system was conditioned to associate relief with substances. When you remove the substance, those circuits don't vanish overnight. They fire as memory traces. The good news? Circuits can be rewired. Each time you surf a craving instead of obeying it, you literally strengthen new neural pathways. It's not just willpower. It's biology in motion.

Reflection Prompts

- What's the most believable lie your cravings tell you?

- What would happen if you didn't believe it for 90 seconds?

- How does your body respond when you prove it wrong?

Closing Thought

Cravings are not the enemy. They are not proof you're broken. They are proof you're human, proof your brain remembers, proof your body is healing.

A craving is a wave. It rises, peaks, and falls.
And every time you ride it without drowning, you prove something powerful:
You are not your craving. You are your choice.

Cravings, Lies & Dopamine - Interrupting the Thought Spiral and Reclaiming Your Power

Chapter 2 – The Loop That Lies

This Chapter Will Cover:

- How cravings morph into self-deception through the "Craving Lie Loop."

- Mapping the cycle: Emotion → Thought → Justification → Action → Shame → Repeat.

- How "just this once" and other self-gaslighting scripts sneak in.

- Differentiating between relapse fantasies and real unmet needs.

CASEL Alignment

- **Self-Awareness:** Identifying craving-driven thought distortions and mapping personal lie loops.

- **Self-Management:** Practicing tools that interrupt the cycle before it reaches action.

- **Responsible Decision-Making:** Distinguishing between unmet needs and relapse fantasies.

The Loop That Lies

Every craving comes with a script. And if you've ever been caught in one, you know how convincing it can be.

The pattern looks like this:

Emotion → Thought → Justification → Action → Shame → Repeat.

You feel restless or sad. That emotion sparks a thought: *"I need something to take the edge off."* Then the justification arrives: *"It's just this once. I've been good. I deserve a break."*

Action follows. You use.

And when it's over, shame slams in like a hammer: *"See, I knew you couldn't do it. You're still the same. You'll never change."*

That shame doesn't end the cycle. It fuels it. Because when shame rises, the urge to escape rises with it. So the cycle begins again.

Plain language: *The Craving Lie Loop is your brain running a con job on itself. It promises relief but sells regret. Over and over again.*

This is the cruelest trick of addiction. Not the substance itself, but the inner lawyer that argues on its behalf. It doesn't scream, it whispers. It doesn't command - it negotiates. And if you don't catch it, you buy the same bad deal again and again.

The good news? Loops can be broken. But only if you name them for what they are.

Why "Just This Once" Is Never Just Once

One of the most dangerous lies in recovery is *"just this once."* It feels harmless. Reasonable. Like a compromise.

You tell yourself:

- *"It's just tonight."*

- *"I'm only taking the edge off."*

- *"Nobody will know."*

- *"I can get right back on track tomorrow."*

But here's the truth: **"just this once" is never about once.** It's about restarting the loop.

When you give in to that lie, you reinforce the craving pathway in your brain. You strengthen the association between discomfort and escape. And most of all, you invite shame back into the driver's seat.

People relapse not because they don't know better, but because they believe the lie that one slip won't matter. And yet, one slip often brings the avalanche.

The danger isn't in the thought itself. The danger is believing it without naming it as a lie.

Plain language: *Cravings whisper lies. The deadliest one is "this doesn't count."*

Relapse Fantasies vs. Unmet Needs

Here's a distinction most people miss: not every craving is about the substance itself. Many are about unmet needs that the substance used to cover.

Example: You feel lonely. The craving shows up, and your brain spins a fantasy: *"If I used right now, I'd feel connected again."* But the need underneath isn't actually for the substance. It's for connection.

Or you're anxious. The fantasy whispers: *"One hit would calm me down."* But the need isn't for the drug, it's for regulation.

This is how cravings hijack real needs and wrap them in lies. The fantasy promises the old shortcut. But the shortcut never works long-term. It just sends you back into the loop.

That's why naming unmet needs matters. It gives you choices. If the need is comfort, you can call a friend. If it's calm, you can breathe, move, stretch, and ground. If it's joy, you can laugh, listen to music, or create.

Plain language: *Relapse fantasies are your brain mislabeling a need. The substance isn't the answer. The need is the answer.*

The Takeaway

Cravings don't just hit your body; they spin a story. The "just this once" loop promises relief but always delivers regret. Every time you buy into the script, shame drives the next round. That cycle can feel airtight, but it isn't. Naming the lie out loud, *this isn't about once, it's about restarting the loop*, breaks its power.

When you catch the unmet need underneath, you turn the craving into a clue instead of a command. Loneliness points to connection. Anxiety points to regulation. Restlessness points to movement. The fantasy isn't the truth, the need is.

Plain language:
Cravings lie. Needs don't. If you can name the need, you can answer it without going back to the loop.

The Spiral That Led to Collapse

Darren was 34, five months clean, and feeling strong. He had a job again. His mom was talking to him. He was going to meetings. Then one Friday night, the craving hit.

He was sitting in traffic, stressed, tired, and lonely. The thought whispered: *"I deserve one night off. Just this once."* By the time he got home, the loop had started.

Emotion: Frustration, fatigue, loneliness.
Thought: *"I need relief."*
Justification: *"I've been good. I can handle it. Nobody will know."*
Action: He called his old contact. Used.
Shame: *"I'm a fraud. I'll never change."*

The next morning, he sat on the edge of his bed, head in his hands. *"All that work, gone."* He almost didn't go back to group. Almost didn't admit it. Almost gave up.

But when he told the story out loud, his counselor said: *"You didn't relapse because you used. You relapsed because you believed the lie before you used."*

That shift mattered. Darren started tracking his Craving Lie Loops. He began catching them earlier, at the thought stage, not the action stage. And slowly, the loop lost its grip.

"CRAVINGS NEVER SCARED ME AS MUCH AS THE LIES I TOLD MYSELF AFTER. 'JUST ONCE.' 'NO ONE WILL KNOW.' 'I DESERVE IT.' THAT WAS THE REAL TRAP, NOT THE CRAVING, BUT THE STORY THAT FOLLOWED IT.

HERE'S THE TRUTH: THE CRAVING WILL PASS ON ITS OWN. THE LIE WANTS TO DRAG YOU BACK. YOUR JOB ISN'T TO FIGHT FOREVER. IT'S JUST TO BREAK THE LOOP IN FRONT OF YOU. ONE INTERRUPTION AT A TIME. THAT'S HOW YOU WIN." **UNCLE A**

Tools & Exercises

Craving Lie Loop Tracker

Purpose: To catch the loop before it reaches behavior.

How to Use It:

1. Draw this cycle: **Emotion → Thought → Justification → Action → Shame**

2. When a craving hits, fill in one word or sentence for each step.

3. Name the lie. (Ex: "Just one won't matter," "I deserve this," "I can stop after today.")

4. Circle the point where you *could have* broken the loop.

Example:

- Emotion: Lonely

- Thought: "Nobody gets me."

- Justification: "I'm better off high than hurt."

- Action: Texted my dealer

- Shame: "I'm back at zero."

Now go back and circle **justification**. That's where the lie lived. And that's where the truth could have stepped in.

Plain Language:
When you map the loop, you stop being its victim. You become its witness. And witnesses don't have to obey the lie.

Emergency Dopamine Reset Menu

Purpose: To redirect the brain when it's chasing fast relief.

How to Use It:
Create a list of **3-5 activities** that give you *real*, if small, relief, without feeding your craving loop. Use this list when your body starts buzzing or your brain starts bargaining.

Examples:

- Hold an ice cube and count backwards from 100.
- Listen to a song you loved before addiction.
- Step outside and name 5 things you can see.
- Send one message to a safe person that says "check in?"
- Write down one truth: "I don't want to go backward."

Why it works:

Your brain wants dopamine. These give it *just enough* to ride the wave without collapsing.

Pro tip:

Keep your list visible. On your wall. In your wallet. On your phone. Train your brain to reach for it automatically.

Exercises

Break the Spiral

Purpose: To stop cravings before they spiral into action.

Steps:

1. Notice the first craving thought. Say out loud: *"This is a craving lie."*

2. Ask: *What do I really need right now?* (Loneliness? Distraction? Comfort?)

3. Choose one action that meets the *real* need.

4. Write the new loop:
   Emotion → Thought → Protective Action → Relief (without shame)

Example:

- Emotion: Anxious

- Thought: "I need a hit to calm down."

- Protective Action: Breathwork + 10 pushups

- Relief: "I made it 20 minutes. That's a win."

Do this daily. The lie gets quieter every time you call it out.

One Lie, One Truth

Purpose: To strengthen truth-telling during craving states.

Steps:

1. Write down the last three craving lies you believed.

   - "I've already messed up, so I might as well."
   - "It's not that big a deal."
   - "I'll stop tomorrow."

2. For each one, write a counter-truth.

   - "I messed up, but I can stop now."
   - "It *is* a big deal, I don't want to live like that."
   - "If I can stop tomorrow, I can stop today."

3. Read the truths out loud every morning this week. Bonus: Record them as voice memos.

Why it matters:

Lies lose power when you name them. Truth gets stronger when you hear it in your own voice.

Build Your Craving Kit

Purpose: To create a physical anchor that interrupts craving momentum.

Steps:

1. Choose 3–5 small, sensory items that calm or ground you.

   - Gum, stress ball, grounding stone, scent oil, index card with a quote

2. Place them in a pouch, zip bag, or dedicated drawer.

3. Label it: *"My Reset Kit."*

4. Every time you feel a craving, use one item for 90 seconds before you decide anything else.

Bonus:

Write a note to yourself and put it inside. Start with:
"Hey, you. If you're holding this, it means the craving showed up. That's okay. You're still in charge. Breathe first."

Dr. Jones' Advisory	Nurse C's Note
Self-gaslighting is a trauma response.	Craving lies often arrive with body cues before thoughts.
Survivors learn to minimize their own needs and justify harmful behaviors as survival strategies.	A tight chest, restless legs, sweaty palms, these are nervous system activations that make the mind scramble for shortcuts.
In recovery, this shows up as relapse rationalization: the brain convincing itself that self-destruction is relief.	Learning to recognize the body's first signs gives you a head start.
Therapy focuses on naming these distortions, reframing them, and teaching clients to validate their needs without shame.	Instead of waiting until the justification shows up, catch the craving in your skin.
The lie loses power once it's exposed to light.	Then apply grounding before the loop gains momentum.

Reflection Prompts

- What's the most common lie my cravings tell me?

- Where in the loop do I usually give in?

- What unmet need do my relapse fantasies point to?

Closing Thought

The craving isn't the problem. The lie is.

The loop will whisper, bargain, justify, seduce. But once you name it, the spell breaks. Every time you catch the lie earlier, you reclaim power.

Remember: the loop is not you. It's a program your brain runs. And like any program, it can be rewritten.

Chapter 3 – Anxiety's Sneaky Role

This Chapter Will Cover:

- How anxiety acts as a craving amplifier, not just background noise.

- Recognizing dread, stress, and fear as direct triggers for relapse urges.

- Body-based resets and interrupters to short-circuit anxiety-driven cravings.

- Differentiating anxiety from depression or withdrawal symptoms.

CASEL Alignment:

- **Self-Awareness**: Identifying anxiety patterns, early body cues, and their relationship to cravings.

- **Self-Management**: Using grounding resets and EMO-PATH™ Core 7 mapping to regulate.

- **Responsible Decision-Making**: Distinguishing fear-driven impulses from safe, protective actions.

- **Relationship Skills**: Communicating anxiety without shame or secrecy.

- **Social Awareness**: Recognizing how anxiety can mask itself in relationships and recovery groups.

The Hidden Hand of Anxiety

Anxiety rarely kicks down the front door. It slips in through cracks, whispering doubts in the back of your mind. Most people in recovery brace for cravings, shame, or loneliness. But what sneaks up most often is anxiety, the relentless hum that makes everything feel unbearable.

Anxiety is sneaky because it doesn't always feel like panic. Sometimes it's racing thoughts that won't stop. Sometimes it's tightness in your chest when nothing "bad" is happening. Sometimes it's the dread of walking into work, the weight of an unanswered text, or the nagging sense that something is wrong even when nothing is.

And here's the trap: anxiety makes cravings louder. It hijacks your nervous system, floods your body with adrenaline, and leaves you desperate for relief. The craving doesn't come out of nowhere, it's anxiety's echo.

Think of it like static on a radio. The song (your real life) is playing, but the static (anxiety) makes it unbearable to hear. And the brain, trained by years of using, remembers there's a button that makes static go away. That button is the substance.

But the static isn't permanent. It can be tuned down. You don't need the old button. You need new tools to lower the volume until you can hear the song again.

Plain language: Anxiety is like your body's alarm system. In recovery, the alarm often gets stuck "on" even when there's no fire.

When Fear Feeds the Craving

Here's the dangerous part: anxiety doesn't just make you uncomfortable. It tricks you into believing relief is impossible without escape.

The thought spiral often looks like this:

- Dread shows up, maybe about money, work, or a conversation you're avoiding.

- Your body reacts, tight chest, sweaty palms, restless legs.

- The craving hits: "If I used, this feeling would disappear."

- You justify: "Just once. Just to calm down. Just to get through today."

- Relief feels urgent, survival-level urgent.

But here's the truth: cravings born from anxiety are not proof you're weak. They're proof your nervous system is dysregulated. Anxiety cranks the volume. The craving is just the echo.

Recovery requires learning how to separate the two. When anxiety starts talking, you don't need to follow it into cravings. You can stop at the source: the fear, the tension, the stress.

That's why grounding resets are critical. Instead of chasing relief through old habits, you use quick body-based interventions to teach your system: "I'm safe right now. I don't need the old escape."

Plain language: A craving caused by anxiety isn't about the substance. It's about your body begging for calm.

The Cycle of Silent Panic

One of the hardest parts of recovery is that anxiety doesn't always show up as obvious panic. It can masquerade as irritability, perfectionism, exhaustion, or even boredom. Many people relapse because they never realized anxiety was the real trigger.

Consider this:

- You snap at someone in traffic.

- You procrastinate on a simple task.

- You feel restless, pacing around the house with no reason.

- You scroll endlessly, avoiding silence.

These look like small behaviors. But they're smoke signals from anxiety. If ignored, they pile up until a craving slams into you out of nowhere. But it wasn't out of nowhere, it was building all along.

That's why tracking anxiety is just as important as tracking cravings. They're linked. Every anxious spiral you map is a craving you may prevent.

This isn't about perfection. It's about awareness. Once you recognize anxiety's fingerprints, you can respond before it snowballs. You can reset before the craving even gets a chance to speak.

The Takeaway

Anxiety doesn't crash in like a craving, it seeps in, rewiring your body to live on edge. That tension makes urges louder, but the substance isn't what you're really chasing. You're chasing calm.

The lie anxiety sells is that relief is impossible without escape. The truth is, relief is possible with grounding, awareness, and new patterns. Tracking the small signals, irritability, procrastination, restlessness, lets you intervene before cravings even arrive.

Plain language:
Cravings born from anxiety aren't about using. They're your body asking for safety. When you tune the static down with healthier tools, you stop mistaking the echo for the answer.

The Spiral Before the Fall

Jordan was 35, nine months clean, and convinced he had recovery under control. He went to meetings, worked his job, kept his routines. But what he didn't notice was the steady creep of anxiety.

It started with sleepless nights. Tossing and turning, heart pounding, replaying conversations in his head. Then came the irritability, snapping at coworkers, picking fights with his partner. He brushed it off: "I'm just stressed."

But under the surface, anxiety was rewiring his cravings. Each sleepless night turned into dread of the next day. Each argument made his chest tighter. Soon, the old thought crept back: "One hit and I'd finally relax."

For weeks, he fought it. He white-knuckled his way through the cravings. He told no one. He thought, "I can handle this."

Then one night, after a brutal shift at work, the spiral snapped. The craving won. And when he relapsed, it wasn't because he "wanted the drug." It was because anxiety had been running the show for weeks.

Looking back, Jordan said, "I thought relapse would be this big dramatic moment. But really, it started the first night I couldn't sleep and told myself I was fine."

That's the sneaky role of anxiety. It builds silently until the craving feels like the only answer.

"ANXIETY WAS MY SHADOW IN RECOVERY. IT FOLLOWED ME EVERYWHERE. I DIDN'T EVEN REALIZE HALF MY CRAVINGS WEREN'T ABOUT THE SUBSTANCE, THEY WERE ABOUT FEAR. FEAR OF FAILING. FEAR OF BEING SEEN. FEAR OF JUST SITTING STILL. WHEN I LEARNED TO NAME MY ANXIETY, MY CRAVINGS FINALLY LOST THEIR BITE. DON'T FIGHT THE SHADOW, TURN AND FACE IT." **UNCLE A**

Tools & Exercises

Grounding Reset Plan

Purpose: To break the anxiety-craving link by calming the body before it spirals.

How to Use It:

1. The moment you feel anxiety rising, **pause**.

2. Name **three things you see**, **two things you hear**, and **one thing you can touch**.

3. **Place both feet flat** on the ground. Press down like you're anchoring into the earth.

4. Breathe out; slow, steady, full exhale.

5. Say out loud: *"I am here. I am safe. This is anxiety, not danger."*

6. Repeat until the craving softens. You don't have to erase it. You just have to survive the peak.

Plain Language:
Anxiety tricks the body into chasing relief. But if you create safety first, your brain stops looking for escape.

EMO-PATH™ Core 7 Anxiety Map

Purpose: To track how anxiety feeds cravings and spot the earliest point of intervention.

How to Use It:

1. Write down one specific moment this week when anxiety spiked.

2. Walk it through the **Core 7**:

   - **Event:** What happened?

   - **Mood:** What emotion hit first?

   - **Thought:** What did your mind tell you?

   - **Body Sensation:** What did you feel physically?

   - **Impulse:** What did you want to do?

   - **Protective Action:** What did you actually do instead (if anything)?

   - **Hopeful Anchor:** What belief or goal helped pull you back?

3. If the **impulse** was a craving, **underline it**. That's your red flag. That's where to interrupt next time.

Plain Language:
Cravings don't show up alone. They ride the back of panic. Mapping your anxiety breaks that ride.

The Anxiety Interrupt

Purpose: To catch anxiety in the body before it turns into craving in the brain.

Steps:

1. Pick a daily routine activity, showering, driving, eating, checking your phone.

2. Use that moment as your **checkpoint**.

3. Pause and scan:

   - Tight chest?
   - Racing thoughts?
   - Jaw clenched?
   - Shoulders high?

4. If yes, pause for 30 seconds and:

   - Stretch.
   - Breathe.
   - Say: *"I'm okay. I can stay."*

5. Afterward, ask: *Did the craving shrink? Did the pressure drop?*

Track your answers for a week. You'll notice your body whispering *before* your brain starts yelling.

Rename the Signal

Purpose: To shift the narrative around anxiety from weakness to warning system.

Steps:

1. Write down 3 recent times you felt "off." Not a full panic attack, just off.

2. For each one, answer:

   - What was my **first physical signal**?

   - What did I **tell myself** it meant?

   - What was it **really trying to warn me about**?

3. Now rename the signal.

    - Example: "I wasn't lazy. I was flooded."

    - "I wasn't mad. I was scared."

    - "I wasn't craving. I was disconnected."

Why it works:
The story you tell yourself during anxiety decides whether you use or stay grounded.

Create a Craving-Safe Zone

Purpose: To reduce craving flare-ups by designing your environment for nervous system safety.

Steps:

1. Pick one small area you control, your nightstand, your car, your phone home screen.

2. Fill it with 3 things that **calm or center you**.

    o   A grounding object

    o   A written reminder (quote, goal, name)

    o   A physical comfort (scent, texture, item)

3. Label that space: *"My Safe Zone"*

4. Use it **only** when cravings or anxiety hit. Train your body to associate it with relief.

Why it matters:
Your nervous system learns through **repetition** and **location**. Give it a place to reset, no substances required.

Dr. Jones' Advisory	Nurse C's Note
Trauma survivors often live with chronic anxiety that blends into daily life.	Anxiety isn't just in your head. It's in your body.
This baseline hypervigilance becomes so normalized that people don't see it as a relapse risk.	Elevated heart rate, shallow breathing, sweaty palms, racing thoughts, these are physiological signals.
But it is. Emotional relapse begins when anxiety goes unnamed.	Many clients think relapse 'just happens,' but I often see weeks of rising anxiety in their body first.
Naming it, tracking it, and treating it as valid is critical. Anxiety isn't weakness. It's a wound.	By noticing these signs, you gain time.
And wounds can heal.	And time gives you choices.

Reflection Prompts

- When was the last time anxiety disguised itself as something else (anger, boredom, fatigue)?

- What cravings have I felt that were actually anxiety in disguise?

- What would change in my recovery if I treated anxiety as a **signal**, not a **weakness**?

Write your answers down. Don't just think them. This is part of your rewiring process.
Your truth on paper becomes your guide out of the fog.

Closing Thought

Anxiety will whisper. It will disguise itself. It will tell you that relief is impossible without escape. But you know better now. The craving is not the problem, the anxiety beneath it is. When you learn to meet anxiety with grounding, awareness, and compassion, you cut the craving at its root.

You are not weak for feeling anxious. You are human. And in recovery, humanity is not a liability. It's your strength.

Chapter 4 – Shame as a Setup

This Chapter Will Cover:

- Why unresolved shame feeds cravings.

- How to distinguish shame from guilt.

- Why shame spirals set the stage for relapse.

- How to reframe shame spirals before they ignite urges.

- A real-world story (Daniel) of collapsing under shame loops.

- Tools for reshaping shame into growth:

- Reflection prompts for naming shame without letting it dominate.

- Insights from Nurse C (body-based shame reactions) and Dr. Jones (trauma shame vs. moral failing).

CASEL Alignment:

- **Self-Awareness:** Naming shame spirals and identifying their triggers.

- **Self-Management:** Using structured worksheets and pauses to disrupt automatic shame responses.

- **Responsible Decision-Making:** Recognizing when guilt is a call to change versus shame being a trap.

Shame Is a Setup, Not the Truth

Shame is one of the most dangerous emotions in recovery because it masquerades as truth. When it shows up, it doesn't whisper, it screams: *"You're broken. You're bad. You'll never be enough."*

Here's the thing: shame isn't a compass. Shame doesn't guide you toward repair. Shame freezes you. It traps you in silence and makes you believe that the damage you caused is permanent.

Guilt, on the other hand, has purpose. Guilt says: *"I did something wrong. I can do better next time."* Shame says: *"I am wrong, and nothing will ever change."*

That difference matters. People relapse not because they don't care, but because shame convinces them there's no point in trying. When you believe you're permanently broken, you stop investing in healing.

In recovery, shame doesn't just follow mistakes, it can appear even on your best days. You might land a job, reconnect with family, or earn trust back, and still the thought sneaks in: *"If they knew the real me, they'd leave."* This is how shame sabotages progress.

Plain language: *Shame is like quicksand. The harder you struggle against it, the deeper you sink. The only way out is to stop treating it like truth and start treating it like a setup.*

The Spiral That Fuels Cravings

Shame doesn't usually show up in isolation. It builds slowly, spiraling through layers:

- You remember something you did.

- That memory triggers disgust or regret.

- Disgust turns inward: *"I'm not just someone who lied. I'm a liar."*

- The spiral grows: *"If I'm a liar, then I'll never be trustworthy again."*

- Despair follows. And despair whispers: *"Why stay clean if you'll never be good enough?"*

That whisper sets the stage for cravings. Cravings don't always come because your body wants the chemical. They come because your mind wants relief from the unbearable weight of shame.

The dangerous part is how convincing shame feels. When anxiety shows up, you know it's a feeling. When sadness shows up, you can often trace it to a loss. But shame feels like reality. It feels like identity. That's why it's lethal.

The truth? Shame is not identity. Shame is a learned reaction, a survival response from trauma, rejection, and mistakes that became internalized. It feels fused to who you are, but it's not permanent.

Plain language: *Shame is a liar that borrows your own voice.*

Reframing Shame Into Motion

You can't just tell yourself to "stop feeling shame." That's like telling someone drowning in water to "just breathe." What you can do is reframe shame before it pulls you under.

Here's how:

- First, name it. When you catch yourself thinking *"I'm bad,"* pause and label it: "This is shame talking."

- Next, separate the action from the identity. Ask yourself: *Did I do something harmful, or am I condemning myself for existing?*

- Finally, replace the judgment with curiosity. Instead of *"I'll never change,"* try: *"What support do I need to act differently next time?"*

The shift is small but powerful. Shame is absolute. Curiosity creates motion. And motion is how you escape the trap.

Reframing isn't pretending you didn't cause harm. It's acknowledging harm while refusing to brand yourself as harm itself. That's how growth happens, not by erasing the past, but by refusing to let shame dictate the future.

The Takeaway

Shame is not a mirror of who you are, it's a trap designed to keep you stuck. It screams louder than guilt, but unlike guilt, it has no direction and no repair in it. Left unchecked, shame spirals into despair and feeds cravings, convincing you that there's no point in trying.

But shame is not identity. It's a learned voice, not a permanent truth. By naming it, separating action from self, and replacing judgment with curiosity, you turn paralysis into motion.

Plain language:
Shame is a setup, not the truth. The more you catch it for what it is, the less power it has to define you, and the freer you are to keep moving forward in recovery.

Daniel's Collapse

Daniel was 41 and six months clean when the shame spiral caught him. He'd been doing well, new job, reconnecting with his brother, showing up for meetings. On the surface, he was thriving.

But one night, alone in his apartment, he opened a drawer and saw an old photo of his daughter. The shame hit like a truck. He remembered missed birthdays, broken promises, nights she cried while he was too high to notice. The memory wasn't just painful, it rewrote his identity in that moment: *"I'm not a dad. I'm a fraud."*

The spiral took over:

- *"I'll never be forgiven."*

- *"She deserves better than me."*

- *"Why even stay clean if I've already failed?"*

By morning, Daniel had called his old dealer. He didn't relapse because he wanted the drug. He relapsed because he wanted a moment without shame.

In treatment afterward, his counselor walked him through the difference between guilt and shame. Guilt could have driven him to repair, to keep showing up for his daughter. Shame told him repair was impossible. That lie was what set him up.

Daniel's story became a turning point in group: naming shame as a relapse trigger, not a personal truth.

> "LISTEN. SHAME WILL TAKE THE SHAPE OF YOUR OWN VOICE. THAT'S WHAT MAKES IT SO DAMN CONVINCING. YOU'LL THINK IT'S YOU TALKING, BUT IT'S NOT. IT'S EVERY OLD WOUND, EVERY MISTAKE, EVERY ECHO OF THE PAST PILING UP IN YOUR HEAD. YOU DON'T FIGHT SHAME BY ARGUING WITH IT. YOU FIGHT IT BY REFUSING TO TAKE ITS VOICE AS GOSPEL. YOU'RE NOT BROKEN. YOU'RE REBUILDING. DON'T LET SHAME TELL YOU OTHERWISE." **UNCLE A**

Tools & Exercises

Shame Reframe Worksheet

Purpose: To separate action from identity and reframe spirals before they ignite cravings.
How to Do It:

1. Write down one recurring shame thought (e.g., "I'm a bad parent").

2. Break it into two parts: What happened (fact) vs. what you tell yourself it means (judgment).

3. Replace the judgment with a new statement focused on possibility (e.g., "I hurt my child, but I'm showing up differently now").

4. Repeat weekly, tracking how your reframes shift over time.

Self-Compassion Pause

Purpose: To interrupt shame in real time with a small act of care.
How to Do It:

1. When shame spikes, pause and place your hand on your chest or stomach.

2. Take three slow breaths.

3. Say one sentence of compassion aloud (e.g., "I'm hurting, but I'm trying.").

4. Notice how your body shifts. Repeat as needed.

Dr. Jones' Advisory	Nurse C's Note
Trauma-based shame is not the same as moral failing. Trauma shame says: *'I am bad because of what happened to me.'* Moral failing says: *'I chose to harm.'* Both can coexist, but untangling them matters. Recovery depends on learning which voice belongs to trauma and which to responsibility. Shame collapses the two into one and leaves no room for growth. Naming the difference is how clients reclaim power.	Shame activates the same stress pathways as physical threat. Heart rate spikes, muscles tense, digestion shuts down. Your body literally thinks you're in danger when shame hits. That's why cravings follow, because the brain looks for quick relief. Pausing, breathing, and grounding aren't just psychological tricks. They're how you calm a nervous system that believes it's under attack.

Reflection Prompt

- What's one thought I carry that's rooted in shame, not truth?

- If I separated the fact from the judgment, what new possibility would open up?

Closing Thought

Shame is not proof of who you are. It's a setup designed to keep you stuck. You are not the spiral. You are the person learning how to climb out of it.

Chapter 5 – Building Your Craving Kit

This Chapter Will Cover:

- Why cravings escalate when we don't have a plan.

- How to design a craving kit that addresses both body and mind.

- The difference between physical anchors (objects, sensory tools) and emotional anchors (reminders, connections).

- How place, time, and trigger type should shape your kit.

- Why shame-free preparation is the opposite of weakness.

CASEL Alignment

- **Self-Awareness:** Naming your triggers and learning how cravings show up in your body.

- **Self-Management:** Building and practicing a personal toolkit to redirect cravings.

- **Responsible Decision-Making:** Choosing preparation over impulse.

- **Relationship Skills:** Incorporating safe supports and shared accountability into your kit.

- **Social Awareness:** Recognizing that cravings are not a moral flaw, but a neurobiological signal.

Cravings Are Predictable If You're Ready

Most people think cravings strike like lightning. Out of nowhere. Unpredictable. Dangerous. But the truth is cravings are patterned. They follow rhythms, time of day, places you walk past, memories that get stirred up.

If you've ever had the same craving every afternoon, or every time you drove past a certain gas station, you already know this. Cravings are not random. They are rehearsed. Your brain learned them over and over, and now they fire like muscle memory.

That's why a craving kit matters. Not because you'll stop every craving forever, but because when one shows up, you've got an answer ready. You don't freeze. You don't panic. You don't white-knuckle it in silence. You reach for your kit and let it carry some of the weight.

Plain language: *A craving kit is a collection of objects, reminders, and practices that interrupt urges in real time.*

Without one, cravings run the show. With one, cravings lose their grip.

Why Preparation Beats Willpower

Here's a dangerous myth: "If I'm strong enough, I won't need help."

That lie kills progress. Cravings are not about strength. They are about circuits in your brain firing like they always have. You don't out-muscle them. You out-prepare them.

Think about it: if a firefighter showed up to a burning building without gear, you wouldn't call them brave. You'd call them reckless. Recovery is no different. Walking into life without tools isn't proof of courage. It's setting yourself up to burn.

When cravings show up, your prefrontal cortex, the rational, decision-making part of your brain, is already hijacked. Blood flow shifts to survival circuits. That means the longer you hesitate, the harder it gets to make a safe choice. Your kit closes that gap.

Your kit does three things:

1. **Interrupts the body loop.** Grounding objects (stone, rubber band, essential oil, ice cube) jolt you out of autopilot.

2. **Calms the nervous system.** Breath scripts, movement drills, or sensory resets slow your physiology before panic peaks.

3. **Refocuses the brain.** Anchors like written affirmations, voice memos from loved ones, or a Core 7 map redirect thoughts into a track that makes sense again.

Plain language: *Preparation isn't weakness. It's strategy. A craving kit is like carrying water in the desert. You don't wait until you're dying of thirst to look for a well.*

This isn't about if you'll need it. You will. The question is whether you'll be ready when the craving rings the bell.

Anchors That Actually Work

Not every anchor works for every person. Some people calm down by touch. Others need sound. Others need movement. That's why your craving kit has to be personal.

There are **two categories of anchors** you'll want to include:

1. **Physical Anchors**, things you can hold, smell, taste, or hear.

   - A smooth stone that you rub in your hand.

   - A peppermint or cinnamon candy that shocks your senses.

   - Headphones and a playlist that shifts your mood.

   - A rubber band to snap gently on your wrist.

   - A grounding scent like lavender oil or eucalyptus.

2. **Emotional Anchors**, reminders that reconnect you to truth.

   - A picture of someone you're healing for.

   - A sticky note with your top 3 reasons to stay clean.

   - A short voice memo to yourself: "Breathe. You've been here before. You're safe."

   - A page from your EMO-PATH™ Core 7 map that shows how you got through last time.

Place, time, and trigger matter too. If your biggest cravings come at night, put your kit by your bed. If it's driving, keep a version in your car. If it's work stress, put one in your desk.

Plain language:
Anchors only work if you can reach them. Your kit should live where your cravings live.

And don't wait until the storm hits to try them. Practice them when you're calm. That way, when the urge comes, your body already knows the drill.

Why Shame-Free Preparation Matters

This is where most people trip: they build a kit, then hide it. They feel embarrassed. Like needing a kit means they're weak, broken, or not "really" in recovery.

But shame is a setup. If you're ashamed of needing tools, you won't use them. And when you don't use them, cravings win.

Think about it: you'd never shame someone for carrying an inhaler. You'd never mock someone for using insulin. A craving kit is no different. It's not proof of weakness. It's proof you're alive, and you're choosing to stay that way.

Shame tells you to fight cravings in silence. Strategy tells you to reach for your anchors.

Here's the truth: cravings don't care if you feel embarrassed. They'll take you out if you're not ready. A craving kit doesn't just interrupt urges. It dismantles shame by proving that preparedness is power.

Plain language: *Shame says, "You should be past this by now." Preparation says, "You're still healing, and that's okay."*

The more openly you use your kit, the less shame sticks. And every time you use it, you're rewriting your story: I'm not weak for needing help. I'm strong because I'm ready.

The Takeaway

Cravings aren't random lightning bolts, they're rehearsed patterns your brain repeats. That's why willpower alone won't save you, but preparation will. A craving kit stocked with anchors gives you quick ways to interrupt the body loop, calm your nervous system, and refocus your mind before the spiral takes over.

When you treat preparation as strength, not shame, you strip cravings of their power. Every time you reach for your kit instead of white-knuckling in silence, you prove to yourself: you're not helpless. You're ready.

Plain language:
Cravings may be predictable, but so is your power, if you prepare for them.

Darren's Commute

Darren was 35, six months clean, and terrified of his commute. Every day, the drive home from work pulled him past his old dealer's street. Every day, the craving hit like a freight train.

At first, Darren tried to power through. He gripped the wheel, clenched his jaw, and told himself, "Be strong." It worked… until the day it didn't. He made the turn and ended up at the corner he swore he'd avoid.

He didn't use that night, but the terror of almost relapsing shook him. His counselor asked: "What's in your craving kit?" Darren admitted he didn't have one. He thought being six months clean meant he should be "past that."

So they built one together:

- A bag of sour candies for shock value.

- A playlist labeled "Drive Home Alive."

- A grounding stone in his cup holder.

- A sticky note on his dashboard: *This craving is 90 seconds. You are longer than that.*

- His daughter's picture tucked in the visor.

The next day, the craving hit. His hands started sweating. The street pulled at him. But instead of gripping the wheel harder, he reached for the kit. Popped a candy. Played the playlist. Rubbed the stone until his pulse slowed.

It didn't erase the craving. But it carried him through the 10 minutes he needed to drive past.

Over time, the kit became second nature. And for Darren, it was the difference between relapsing on a random Tuesday and stacking another month clean.

"DON'T LET SHAME KEEP YOU FROM BEING READY. I'D RATHER LOOK SILLY CHEWING ON SOUR CANDY OR CLUTCHING A ROCK THAN LOOK MY DAUGHTER IN THE EYES AND EXPLAIN WHY I USED AGAIN. TOOLS DON'T MAKE YOU WEAK. THEY MAKE YOU DANGEROUS TO CRAVINGS." **UNCLE A**

Tools & Exercises

Craving Kit Blueprint

Purpose: To design a personal kit that actually works in the moments you need it.
Steps:

1. List your top 3 craving triggers (time, place, emotion).

2. Pick 2 physical anchors and 2 emotional anchors that would interrupt each.

3. Assemble portable versions (bag, car, desk, nightstand).

4. Practice using them at least once when calm.

Anchor Mapping Chart

Purpose: To identify which types of anchors (touch, taste, sound, sight, smell) calm you fastest.
Steps:

1. Make five columns labeled: Touch, Taste, Sound, Sight, Smell.

2. Under each, write 2–3 grounding options.

3. Test each during mild stress to see what calms you fastest.

4. Put the top 2 from each category in your kit.

EMO-PATH™ Core 7 Trigger Map

Purpose: To track the emotional sequence that leads to cravings so you can place your kit where it counts.
Steps:

1. Write down a recent craving.

2. Fill in the Core 7: Event, Mood, Thought, Body Sensation, Impulse, Protective Action, Hopeful Anchor.

3. Circle the point where the craving peaked.

4. Place a tool from your kit at that exact stage (e.g., playlist if it peaked in Thought, stone if it peaked in Body Sensation).

Exercises

The Three-Anchor Drill

Purpose: Train your body and mind to rely on multiple types of anchors during cravings.
How to Do It:

1. Pick one physical anchor (stone, candy, scent).

2. Pick one emotional anchor (photo, note, voice memo).

3. Pick one Core 7 anchor (map, chart, written pattern).

4. Carry them with you for a week.

5. Each time a craving shows up, test all three and note which one helps most.

Personalize Your Tools

Purpose: Strengthen the emotional impact of your kit by attaching meaning to each item.
How to Do It:

1. Choose each item in your craving kit.

2. Write a short note to yourself about its purpose.
   • Example: "This candy isn't candy, it's my reset button."

3. Keep the notes with the items or read them when using the tool.

Emergency Drill

Purpose: Build confidence using your craving kit under pressure.
How to Do It:

1. Set a timer for 90 seconds.

2. Pretend a craving just hit.

3. Use only the items in your kit until the timer ends.

4. Afterward, adjust: Which tools landed hardest? Which ones need replacing or strengthening?

Dr. Jones' Advisory	Nurse C's Note
Shame-driven cravings are powerful because they target your identity. They whisper: 'You're weak for needing help.' That's trauma talking, not truth. A craving kit is a direct intervention, it replaces shame spirals with a practiced, predictable response. Over time, this rewires not just behavior, but identity itself.	Your nervous system needs tangible signals to shift states. Don't underestimate how a sour taste, a cold object, or a grounding scent can reset adrenaline and cortisol in seconds. These sensory tools work with your body, not against it. Your kit is physiology in practice.

Reflection Prompts

- What items already help me reset that I could include in my kit?

- Where do my cravings hit hardest, and how can my kit live there?

- What story do I want my kit to tell about me when I reach for it?

Closing Thought

Your cravings will not wait for you to be ready. They will show up on a Tuesday morning, in traffic, at a birthday party, or in the middle of a fight. You cannot stop them from knocking. But with a craving kit, you don't have to open the door.

Preparedness is not weakness. It is survival, strategy, and strength. Every time you use your kit, you're proving that cravings don't command you, you command your recovery.

Chapter 6 – Surf the Urge, Don't Drown

This Chapter Will Cover

- Explaining urge surfing (DBT, ACT roots).

- The science of cravings as waves, not commands.

- Scripts for narrating cravings out loud to reduce their grip.

- Red/Yellow/Green craving states (STOPLIGHT method).

- Practical drills for riding out urges without collapse.

- successful craving wave navigation.

CASEL Alignment

- **Self-Awareness:** Naming craving states (Green/Yellow/Red).

- **Self-Management:** Practicing urge surfing instead of reacting.

- **Social Awareness:** Understanding how cravings affect relationships.

- **Relationship Skills:** Using scripts to reach for support.

- **Responsible Decision-Making:** Choosing protective action in the "wave."

The Nature of the Wave

One of the hardest truths in recovery is this: cravings don't disappear just because the substance is gone. They show up uninvited, in the middle of a workday, while you're folding laundry, when you're celebrating something good. And when they hit, the instinct is to panic: *Why am I still feeling this? Haven't I come far enough?*

The science says otherwise. A craving is not proof you're failing; it's proof your brain remembers. Decades of research in DBT (Dialectical Behavior Therapy) and ACT (Acceptance and Commitment Therapy) frame cravings as waves. They rise, peak, and fall. The average craving surge, even a strong one, rarely lasts more than two minutes at its highest intensity.

Think about the ocean. If you stand frozen in front of a wave, it crashes into you and knocks you down. If you turn your back and pretend it isn't coming, it will drag you under. But if you learn to surf, to meet it head-on, float with its pull, and ride it until it loses strength, you come out standing. That is what urge surfing teaches: not control, not suppression, but survival without collapse.

The first skill is noticing. You can't surf a wave you refuse to see. The second is staying put. Most people relapse in the first 90 seconds because they assume the wave will get worse forever. But like any wave, cravings break. They do not go on endlessly. When you begin to experience cravings as temporary, as data rather than destiny, your power shifts. You stop drowning. You start riding.

Scripts That Break the Spiral

The urge doesn't just live in the body; it talks in your head. It whispers, *Just this once. You deserve it. No one will know. You're not strong enough anyway.* That inner voice isn't reason, it's panic dressed up as logic. Left unchecked, those thoughts create the spiral that leads from craving to relapse.

This is where narration comes in. Speaking the craving aloud, either to yourself, a journal, or a safe peer, interrupts the loop. When you say, *"My body wants the drug right now. This doesn't mean I'm failing. This is a craving wave, and it will pass,"* something powerful happens. You separate identity from urge. You stop being the craving. You start being the one noticing the craving.

Scripts are not busywork. They are survival. The prefrontal cortex, the part of your brain that handles logic and choice, goes dim when cravings fire. Language reignites it. That's why reading, journaling, and especially speaking re-activate control. Every time you narrate the urge, you buy yourself distance from it.

Think of it like breaking a hypnotist's spell. The craving says, *obey.* Your voice says, *observe.* That simple shift, from blind reaction to spoken awareness, keeps you grounded long enough for the wave to crest and fall. And the more you practice, the easier it becomes. You start to trust the truth: no craving, no matter how strong, has to own you.

The STOPLIGHT Method

Even with science and scripts, cravings can feel overwhelming. That's why the STOPLIGHT Method exists: a fast, visual way to check where you are and what to do.

- **Green:** You feel a light craving, a flicker of memory, a passing thought. At this stage, small actions work: a sip of water, a deep breath, a song that resets your focus.

- **Yellow:** Intensity builds. You notice agitation, racing thoughts, maybe a little sweat or restlessness. This is the danger zone. Here you activate your surfing plan: speak the script, ride the wave, set a two-minute timer, and breathe through it.

- **Red:** The craving feels unbearable. Your body screams for relief. This is the emergency state. The plan here is full protocol: call a support person, use grounding objects from your craving kit, move your body, or leave the trigger environment. The goal is not to "win" the wave but to outlast it safely.

The STOPLIGHT Method works because it normalizes gradations. Instead of "I'm fine" or "I'm relapsing," it gives you a middle ground, and middle ground saves lives. Naming where you are creates choice. And choice is what cravings try to steal.

Mark's First Wave

Mark had been clean for five months when his girlfriend ended their relationship over text. He was blindsided. The loneliness slammed him so hard he almost grabbed his keys and drove straight to his old dealer. His chest felt heavy, his hands shook, and the thought repeated: *One night won't matter. Just one.*

But in his pocket was a card from group: the STOPLIGHT Method. He rated himself Yellow. Instead of obeying the craving, he sat down and read aloud the script he had practiced: *"This is a craving. It's not destiny. It will pass."*

He set a two-minute timer. At first, it was torture. His body screamed louder. His mind yelled, *You're wasting time, just go.* But 90 seconds later, something shifted. His chest loosened. The thought lost volume. By the time the timer went off, the craving had dropped by half. He opened his journal and logged the moment in his Urge Surf Log.

That night, Mark didn't relapse. It wasn't heroic. It was survival, one wave at a time. And that win gave him evidence to trust the next time cravings crashed in.

LET ME TELL YOU THIS STRAIGHT: CRAVINGS ARE NOT PROOF YOU'RE BROKEN. THEY'RE PROOF YOU'RE ALIVE. I USED TO THINK EVERY CRAVING MEANT I WAS WEAK, THAT I WAS DOOMED TO GO BACK. BUT CRAVINGS DON'T MEAN YOU'RE FAILING, THEY MEAN YOUR BRAIN REMEMBERS. THAT'S ALL.

THE TRICK ISN'T TO KILL CRAVINGS. YOU CAN'T. THE TRICK IS TO RIDE THEM LONG ENOUGH TO SEE THAT THEY DIE ON THEIR OWN. EVERY WAVE I SURFED WAS ONE LESS RELAPSE. AND EVERY TIME I MADE IT THROUGH, I BUILT A RECEIPT: PROOF THAT I COULD. KEEP STACKING THOSE RECEIPTS. ONE DAY, THE WAVES DON'T SCARE YOU ANYMORE. **UNCLE A**

Tools & Exercises

STOPLIGHT Method Card

Purpose: To build real-time craving awareness and guide immediate action based on risk level.

How to Use It:

1. Make a small card or note on your phone with three sections:

    - **Green** – Low-risk craving. You're aware but grounded.

        Action: Drink water, do a grounding breath, name what you're feeling.

- 🟡 **Yellow** – Medium risk. You're agitated, triggered, or justifying use.

  Action: Text a support person. Step outside. Use a grounding tool.

- 🔴 **Red** – High-risk. You're spiraling, making plans, or ready to use.

  Action: Remove yourself from the setting. Use your emergency plan. Call for help.

2. Carry it everywhere. Pull it out the *second* a craving hits.

Why It Works:

Cravings make you forget your tools. This card makes the tools automatic, no thinking, just action.

Urge Surf Log

Purpose: To track the rise, peak, and fall of cravings, proving they pass.

How to Use It:

1. Set up a notebook or digital note with these headers:

   - Trigger
   - Craving intensity (1–10)
   - Body sensations
   - Action taken
   - Duration
   - How it ended

2. Fill it in every time you feel a craving, even if small.

3. Review it weekly. Look for patterns: certain times, locations, emotions?

Why It Works:

Cravings feel endless. This tool shows you they're not. With data, you'll see your wins, and plan for weak spots.

Guided Urge Surfing Drill

Purpose: To physically practice riding out a craving, building brain-body endurance.

Steps:

1. Set a timer for 90 seconds.

2. Imagine a craving is hitting. (Choose one that's familiar to you.)

3. Say aloud:

   - "This is a craving. It's not an emergency."
   - "I've felt this before. It won't last forever."

4. Track sensations in your body: tension, heartbeat, restlessness.

5. Let the wave rise, crest, and fall. Breathe. When the timer ends, write:

    - What did I feel?
    - What helped me stay?
    - How would I rate my urge now (0–10)?

Why It Works:
You're training your nervous system to *feel and stay*, instead of *feel and flee*.

Craving Narration Script

Purpose: To rewrite the inner monologue of a craving, giving you control of the story.

Steps:

1. Write a short script to say out loud when a craving hits:

    - "I'm not broken. This is a brain loop. It'll pass."
    - "Craving means my brain is reaching for what's familiar, not what's best."
    - "I choose my future, not my past."

2. Practice this script daily, *even when you're not craving.* Say it in the mirror. Whisper it before bed.

Why It Works:
Repetition rewires the brain. When the moment hits, you'll already know the lines.

Daily Craving State Map

Purpose: To build end-of-day awareness and reinforce progress tracking.

Steps:

1. Before bed, ask yourself:

    - Did I have a craving today?
    - Was it Green, Yellow, or Red?
    - What helped? What didn't?

2. Record your response in a journal, notes app, or recovery tracker.

3. Review after 7 days. Celebrate trends. Identify your Yellow triggers before they turn Red.

Why It Works:
Consistency builds confidence. When you track your cravings honestly, you train yourself to *respond*, not *react*.

Dr. Jones' Advisory	Nurse C's Note
Clinically, cravings are not just chemical. They're trauma echoes. The brain remembers relief, and in moments of pain, it demands it again. What's dangerous is not the craving itself, but the shame story attached: *If I still crave, I must not be healed.* That belief drives relapse. Urge surfing reframes cravings as expected, temporary, and survivable. It gives clients agency where trauma once took it away. The key is practice outside of crisis, so when the Red zone hits, the body already knows what to do.	Your body treats cravings like emergencies. Heart rate spikes, adrenaline floods, cortisol rises. That's why cravings feel like danger, even when you're safe. The STOPLIGHT Method works because naming the state signals your nervous system to stand down. Breathing, speaking, and mapping the urge shift you out of panic mode and back into regulation. Remember: cravings are stress responses. Ride them with care, and your nervous system learns they're survivable.

Reflection Prompts

- What did my last craving feel like in my body?

- Which STOPLIGHT state do I usually live in?

- What script feels real to me, one I'll actually say out loud?

- Who can I call if I hit Red?

- How will I remind myself that cravings always end?

Closing Thought

Cravings are not commands. They are waves. You don't drown by feeling them. You drown by fighting them or following them. Learn to surf the urge, and you'll walk out of every craving with proof that you can stand.

Chapter 7 – Dopamine Isn't the Devil

This Chapter Will Cover:

- Why dopamine is not your enemy, it's your survival chemistry.

- The "flatline" in recovery: why joy feels distant and muted.

- How dopamine misfires during substance use and recalibrates afterward.

- The difference between craving dopamine and craving substances.

- How to rebuild a healthy reward system with small, consistent actions.

CASEL Alignment

- **Self-Awareness:** Recognizing flatness and low pleasure as part of recovery, not failure.

- **Self-Management:** Using trackers and gradual reintroduction of joy to rebuild the brain's reward system.

- **Responsible Decision-Making:** Distinguishing between healthy dopamine pursuits and relapse triggers.

- **Relationship Skills:** Sharing small joy practices with others for accountability and connection.

- **Social Awareness:** Understanding that recovery is not about rejecting pleasure, but about learning to embrace it safely.

Why Dopamine Matters

People talk about dopamine like it's the villain. You hear it everywhere: *"Dopamine is addictive." "Dopamine is the problem."* But that's not true. Dopamine isn't the enemy. It's the messenger. It's your brain's way of saying: *That mattered. Let's do it again.*

Every survival behavior you've ever had is tied to dopamine. Eating food. Finding shelter. Connecting with people. Learning a skill. Even laughing at a dumb joke. Dopamine isn't just pleasure, it's motivation. It drives you toward things that keep you alive.

The problem shows up when substances hijack the system. Substances don't just give you a nudge, they slam your reward pathways with tidal waves of artificial dopamine. The spike is so massive that everyday life can't compete. A hug feels flat. A sunrise feels like nothing. Music lands hollow. Not because those things lost meaning, but because your brain adapted. It turned down the volume on natural pleasures just to protect itself from overload.

Plain language: dopamine isn't broken. Substances just stole the steering wheel.

The Flatline Isn't Forever

Here's the stage almost no one prepares you for: the flatline. You wake up, make coffee, eat breakfast, and it all feels gray. Friends laugh and it sounds far away. Music plays but you feel disconnected. Even small wins, a clean day, a safe choice, land hollow.

This is when the mind whispers: *Maybe joy is gone for good. Maybe this is permanent.*

But the flatline isn't proof you're broken. It's your brain's reset mode.

Inside, your dopamine receptors are recalibrating after years of bombardment. Your baseline of pleasure got pushed so high that ordinary life feels like cardboard in comparison. It takes weeks, sometimes months, for receptors to stabilize. Think of it like your ears ringing after a concert. Normal sound feels muted, not because your ears are dead, but because they're adjusting after overload.

The same thing is happening in your nervous system. Flatness isn't emptiness. It's repair. And while it feels unbearable, it's also proof that healing is underway.

Plain language: silence in your reward system doesn't mean the lights are out. It means the wiring is reconnecting.

Rebuilding a Reward System

Here's the hard truth: recovery doesn't give you fireworks. It gives you flickers. Small sparks of joy, subtle enough that you'll miss them if you're not paying attention. The first belly laugh. The first time music makes you move. The first moment you realize, *I'm proud of myself.*

Those flickers are the building blocks. Your brain won't relearn joy through one big event. It relearns through thousands of small sparks stacked together.

That means you need to practice noticing. Every time you choose a walk, cook a meal, call a safe friend, or try something new, you're teaching your brain: *This matters. Do it again.* Over time, the sparks become steady light.

This isn't about forcing happiness. It's about creating space where joy can creep back in, not dramatic, not loud, but real.

Plain language:
Recovery joy doesn't roar. It tiptoes. Your job is to notice.

The Takeaway

Dopamine is not your enemy. It's your fuel. Substances hijacked it, rewired it, and left your brain scorched. The flatline that follows isn't proof of damage beyond repair, it's proof of recalibration. Your nervous system is learning to trust ordinary life again.

You won't feel joy rush in all at once. You'll feel flickers, tiny sparks that seem too small to matter. They matter. Those sparks are the scaffolding of your new reward system.

The takeaway is this: flatness is not forever. It's the rebuilding stage. Stay present long enough to notice the flickers. They are your proof that life is returning.

Marisol's Return to Joy

Marisol was 41, almost a year clean, and ready to give up. She wasn't using, but she wasn't living either. Every day felt flat. She worked, ate, slept, and repeated.

One night, sitting with her counselor, she said: "If this is sobriety, I don't want it. I'd rather feel something, even if it kills me."

Her counselor didn't argue. She gave Marisol an assignment: *Track three sparks every day. Nothing dramatic. Just three moments where something felt less than awful.*

At first, Marisol resisted. "Nothing feels good." But she tried anyway.

- Day one: "My tea was warm."

- Day two: "A stranger smiled at me."

- Day three: "My dog wagged his tail when I got home."

The list felt pathetic. But after two weeks, she noticed she had 42 entries. And looking at them together, she realized something: she wasn't flat all the time.

Her sparks grew: "I laughed at a joke." "I cooked a real dinner." "I woke up without panic."

Marisol didn't find fireworks. She found flickers. And the flickers stacked into something she hadn't felt in years: hope.

"I REMEMBER THINKING MY JOY WAS GONE FOR GOOD. MUSIC DIDN'T HIT. FOOD TASTED LIKE CARDBOARD. I THOUGHT: MAYBE THIS IS JUST WHO I AM NOW. BUT THEN ONE DAY, I LAUGHED AT A DUMB JOKE ON TV. AND IT WASN'T FAKE. IT WAS SMALL. BUT IT WAS REAL. AND THAT'S WHEN I KNEW: JOY WASN'T DEAD. IT WAS JUST WAITING FOR ME TO NOTICE." **UNCLE AARON**

Tools & Exercises

Dopamine Balance Tracker

Purpose: To track small sparks of pleasure over time so your brain can register progress.
How to Do It:

1. Create a chart with columns for Date, Activity, Spark (Y/N), and Rating (0–10).

2. Each day, record at least one activity and whether it gave you a spark.

3. Over weeks, review your chart. Look for gradual increases in "yes" moments.
   Tip: Don't expect 10/10 joy. Even a 2/10 spark is a win.

EMO-PATH™ Core 7 Pleasure Map

Purpose: To map the emotional, physical, and cognitive shifts that happen when small joys return.
How to Do It:

1. Choose one spark moment this week.

2. Fill the Core 7:

   - Event: What happened?

   - Mood: What did you label it?

   - Thought: What ran through your mind?

   - Body Sensation: How did your body react?

   - Impulse: What did you want to do?

   - Protective Action: What safe step did you take?

   - Hopeful Anchor: What does this tell you about your healing?

3. Keep one Pleasure Map per week. Over time, you'll see how joy builds back.

Pleasure Reintroduction List

Purpose: To rebuild your brain's relationship with ordinary joy.
How to Do It:

1. Make a list of 10 activities you used to enjoy before substances.

2. Rank them from easiest to hardest to try again.

3. Pick one "easy" activity each week and do it, no matter how flat it feels.

4. Record how it felt before, during, and after.

5. Revisit harder items as your spark returns.

Exercises

The 10-Minute Joy Test

Purpose: Teach your brain that small, ordinary activities can spark pleasure again.

How to Do It:

1. Pick one simple activity: a walk, music, tea, sketching, journaling, or stretching.

2. Set a timer for **10 minutes**. Commit to staying with the activity, even if you feel flat.

3. When the timer ends, write **one word** about the experience (calm, annoyed, curious, lighter, nothing).

4. Track your words over time to see shifts in how joy begins to return.

Spark Jar

Purpose: Build visible proof that joy is returning, even when flatness convinces you otherwise.

How to Do It:

1. Every time you notice a **spark**, a laugh, a smile, a peaceful moment, a good song, write it on a slip of paper.

2. Drop it in a jar, box, or envelope.

3. When discouragement hits ("nothing's changing"), open the jar and read a few sparks.

Joy Exposure Therapy

Purpose: Retrain your nervous system to trust joy by repeating safe, positive experiences.

How to Do It:

1. Choose **one joy activity per week** (same song, same meal, same walk, same practice).

2. Repeat it at least three times during the week.

3. Pay attention to how familiarity changes the experience over time.

Dr. Jones' Advisory	Nurse C's Note
Trauma and shame often distort dopamine recovery. Survivors may fear joy, associating it with vulnerability or loss. They may sabotage sparks because pleasure feels unsafe. Clinically, it's important to normalize joy as survival, not indulgence. Tracking sparks through structured tools helps clients integrate positive affect into identity, not reject it as a threat.	Dopamine repair doesn't happen overnight. The nervous system can take 6–18 months to recalibrate, depending on the substance and history. Nutrition matters: protein supports dopamine precursors, omega-3s repair receptor health, and hydration stabilizes mood. Movement and sunlight speed recovery. Expect flatness but know it's not permanent. Each spark proves your system is rewiring.

Reflection Prompts

- What moments in my day feel less flat, even if only by a little?

- How can I track sparks so I don't dismiss them?

- What old joys am I willing to reintroduce, even if they feel different now?

Closing Thought

Dopamine isn't the devil. It's the signal that life is worth living. Substances hijacked it, but recovery reclaims it. The flatline is not forever. Sparks stack into flickers. Flickers grow into warmth. And warmth, with patience, grows into joy that lasts.

You are not broken. Your brain is healing. And every spark you notice is proof.

Chapter 8 – Craving ≠ Command

This Chapter Will Cover:

- Why cravings are part of recovery, not proof of relapse or failure.

- How to predict craving patterns and understand urge frequency.

- Reframing cravings as signals, not commands.

- Anchoring relapse prevention in identity, not just willpower.

CASEL Alignment

- **Self-Awareness:** Recognizing cravings as neurological and emotional, not moral failings.

- **Self-Management:** Using structured protocols to track and interrupt craving cycles.

- **Responsible Decision-Making:** Learning to respond to cravings with strategy instead of impulse.

- **Relationship Skills:** Sharing craving management strategies with peers, sponsors, or support networks.

- **Social Awareness:** Understanding that cravings are universal in recovery, reducing stigma and shame.

Cravings Are Not Commands

There's a dangerous lie in recovery culture: *If you crave, you're failing.* That belief keeps people stuck in shame.

Here's the truth: cravings are not proof of weakness. They're proof that your brain remembers. That's all.

When you were using, your brain built strong pathways: *This is how we handle stress, this is how we handle boredom, this is how we numb pain.* Those loops don't vanish the day you quit. They fire automatically when the right trigger shows up.

That doesn't mean relapse is inevitable. It means your nervous system is pulling up an old file. The craving is a suggestion, not a sentence.

Think of it like a pop-up ad on your computer. It shows up because of past clicks. But just because it's there doesn't mean you have to click it.

Plain language: a craving is a suggestion, not a command.

The critical shift is this: when you believe cravings equal relapse, you panic. And panic makes the craving feel louder. But when you treat cravings like noise, background static, not orders, you take away their power.

Predicting the Pattern

Cravings aren't random. They follow rhythms, and once you see the pattern, you stop being surprised by them. And when cravings stop feeling like surprise attacks, they become manageable.

The rhythms usually fall into a few categories:

- **Times of day.** Evening after work. Late nights when you're alone. Early mornings when anxiety peaks.
- **Emotional states.** Anger, sadness, grief, stress, boredom, even celebration.
- **Physical states.** Hunger, fatigue, dehydration, hormonal cycles.
- **Places.** Passing the liquor store, sitting in your car, walking through an old neighborhood.
- **Anniversaries.** Birthdays, losses, clean dates, traumatic anniversaries.

Your brain is wired to link certain cues with past behavior. That's why you feel the pull in the same places, at the same times, under the same emotions.

And this is why journaling matters. You're not just writing feelings for the sake of writing. You're mapping the battlefield. Every entry shows you when and where cravings strike. And once you can predict the pattern, you can plan your response before the urge even shows up.

Plain language: a craving is less dangerous when you know when it's coming.

Identity Anchors Beat Willpower

Here's why white-knuckling doesn't work: willpower gets tired. Identity doesn't.

If your only plan is *"say no harder,"* eventually exhaustion wins. Willpower is like holding your breath, it works for a little while, but eventually the pressure breaks through.

Identity, though, is stronger. When your sense of self shifts, the craving no longer fits who you are.

Identity anchors are truths you can return to in the moment of urge:

- *"I'm a parent who shows up."*

- *"I'm someone who heals, not hides."*

- *"I don't need the old survival strategy. I've built new ones."*

- *"That's not me anymore."*

Willpower says: *I shouldn't use.*
Identity says: *That's not who I am anymore.*

That shift changes everything. When identity grows louder, cravings grow quieter.

Plain language:
Cravings get weaker when your identity gets louder.

The Takeaway

Cravings are not commands. They are echoes of old survival strategies, not verdicts on who you are today. They rise and fall in predictable patterns, and when you track those rhythms, you remove the element of surprise.

More importantly, recovery isn't about endless willpower, it's about anchoring in a new identity. When you know who you are, the craving no longer makes sense.

The takeaway is this: cravings are background noise. They don't decide for you. When you know their pattern and answer with identity instead of panic, you stop being at their mercy.

Devon's Two Minutes

Devon was 35, nine months sober, and sick of fighting cravings. Every night around 10 p.m., the urge hit like clockwork. He white-knuckled until midnight, collapsed in bed, and did it again the next day.

One night, exhausted, he remembered something from group: "A craving isn't a command. It's a wave. Waves pass."

So instead of panicking, he tried something different. He set a timer for two minutes. He told himself: "You don't have to get through the night. Just get through two minutes."

The craving surged. His chest tightened. His brain screamed: "Go get it." He grabbed his worksheet and wrote down the trigger (loneliness), the thought ("This will fix it"), and the anchor ("I'm a father. I don't disappear on my kids anymore.").

By the time the timer buzzed, the craving had dipped. Not gone, but weaker. He set another two minutes. And another. Until it was midnight again.

Devon didn't beat the craving with superhuman willpower. He beat it with two minutes of strategy, repeated until the wave passed.

"I'VE HAD CRAVINGS THAT FELT LIKE THEY WERE GOING TO RIP ME APART. BUT EVERY TIME I RODE ONE OUT, I REALIZED THE SAME THING: THE CRAVING DIDN'T HAVE THE WHEEL. IT SHOUTED, BUT I STILL GOT TO STEER. THAT'S THE TRUTH I WANT YOU TO HOLD ON TO: CRAVINGS AREN'T COMMANDS. THEY'RE NOISE. AND NOISE FADES." **UNCLE A**

Tools & Exercises

Craving Protocol Worksheet

Purpose: To turn cravings from panic moments into structured choices.
How to Do It:

1. When a craving hits, write down:

   - Trigger (What set it off?)
   - Thought (What's running through your mind?)
   - Body Sensation (What's happening physically?)
   - Impulse (What do you want to do?)
   - Anchor (What identity truth are you standing on?)

2. Review after the craving passes. Notice patterns.

Triggers → Response → Anchor Practice

Purpose: To practice interrupting cravings with pre-decided responses.
How to Do It:

1. List three common triggers.

2. For each trigger, write your response. (Example: "When I feel lonely, I text my support buddy.")

3. Attach each response to an anchor. ("I text because I'm someone who doesn't disappear.")

4. Practice weekly until the script feels automatic.

Craving Frequency Journal

Purpose: To map craving rhythms over time.
How to Do It:

1. Each day, log when cravings hit, how strong they felt (0–10), and how long they lasted.

2. Review weekly. Notice patterns.

3. Share trends with your counselor, group, or sponsor.

Exercises

Two-Minute Wave Ride

Purpose: Train your nervous system to recognize that cravings crest and fall like waves.

How to Do It:

1. When the craving hits, don't argue with it. Instead, set a timer for **two minutes**.

2. Plant your feet on the floor. Drop your shoulders. Breathe into your belly, slow, steady, exhaling longer than you inhale.

3. Choose one grounding action: press your palms together, hold an ice cube, or stretch your arms overhead.

4. Stay present until the timer ends. Notice how the urge changes in intensity, it might spike, shift, or soften.

Afterward, ask yourself: *Did the craving feel permanent at first? How did it feel after two minutes?* Write down the change.

Anchor Affirmation Rehearsal

Purpose: Build identity-based reflexes that speak louder than cravings.

How to Do It:

1. Choose one **identity anchor** that feels true and motivating. Examples:

   - "I am someone who heals, not hides."
   - "I'm a parent who shows up."
   - "I am more than my urge."

2. Speak it aloud **three times a day**: morning, midday, and before bed.

3. Bonus: Write it on a sticky note and place it where cravings hit hardest (car, mirror, fridge).

At the end of the week, write: *When did I actually use this anchor during a craving? Did it feel mechanical, or did it shift something inside me?*

Safe Substitution Drill

Purpose: Replace old craving loops with safe, life-giving responses.

How to Do It:

1. Create a **menu of substitutions** that hit different needs:

   - Comfort → Wrap in a blanket, drink tea, or call a safe friend.
   - Energy → Put on music and dance for one song.
   - Calm → Take a shower, step outside, or practice deep breathing.
   - Connection → Send a text that says, "Wave hit. Just checking in."

2. Keep the list visible (phone note, journal, index card).

3. Each time a craving shows up, choose a substitution immediately. Don't debate. Just act.

After using a substitution, rate your craving on a scale of 1–10. Over time, track how fast the numbers drop.

Dr. Jones' Advisory	Nurse C's Note
Cravings are opportunities for identity consolidation. When clients choose not to obey the urge, they reinforce: 'I am not who I was.' Each resisted craving strengthens neural pathways tied to recovery identity. Clinically, cravings should be reframed as practice, not punishment. Each wave survived is integration in action.	Cravings are not random. They follow neurological and hormonal rhythms. Dopamine dips, cortisol spikes, and fatigue cycles all influence urge intensity. Most cravings last 90–120 seconds if not fueled by panic or shame. Hydration, protein, and sleep are crucial, physical stability reduces craving frequency. Remember: your body is recalibrating. Don't confuse chemistry with character.

Reflection Prompts

- When cravings hit, do I treat them as destiny or as noise?
- What patterns do I see in my cravings (times, emotions, places)?
- What identity anchors can I hold on to when willpower runs thin?

Closing Thought

Cravings are not commands. They're echoes of old pathways, noise from a brain that remembers but doesn't decide. Your identity is louder. Your strategy is stronger. Every craving survived is not just proof of willpower, it's proof of who you're becoming.

You are not failing. You are practicing. And every practice makes you freer.

Chapter 9 – Reflection: Cravings as Teachers

This Chapter Will Cover:

- Why cravings are not just obstacles but information.

- How looking back reveals triggers, times, and thought patterns.

- Why reflection transforms scattered moments into a roadmap.

- Tools for mapping cravings and reframing them as guides.

CASEL Alignment:

- **Self-Awareness:** Identifying thought, body, and behavior patterns in cravings.

- **Self-Management:** Using reflection maps to regulate responses instead of reacting.

- **Responsible Decision-Making:** Turning urges into insight that strengthens relapse prevention.

Cravings as Messages, Not Monsters

The first time you feel a craving, it's easy to panic: *This is the enemy. This is the thing that will break me.* For months, maybe years, people told you cravings meant danger, that they were proof you weren't strong enough, that they were the red flag before relapse.

But here's the reframe cravings are not monsters. They are messengers.

A craving is your body and brain saying, *"Something is out of balance. Something needs attention."* It may be exhaustion. It may be loneliness. It may be shame. It may even be joy that feels too big for you to hold. But it's never just about the substance.

Reflection reveals this. It shows you cravings are mirrors, not verdicts. They don't invent needs, they expose them. Every time you've wanted to use again, there was a driver beneath it. Stress. Hunger. Fear. Celebration. When noticed, these drivers can be mapped, studied, and understood.

Plain language:
Cravings aren't monsters hiding under the bed. They're notes from your nervous system. You don't have to fear them. You have to read them.

When you stop running and start reflecting, you take what used to terrify you and turn it into a source of intelligence. Instead of asking *"Why me?"* you begin to ask: *"What is this showing me?"*

Patterns You Miss Until You Look

In the middle of recovery, cravings can feel chaotic. One day you're strong. The next day a stupid argument wrecks you. The day after that, you're fine again. It feels random, like you're being yanked around by invisible strings.

But when you step back and reflect, a pattern emerges.

Look at your last ten cravings. Without reflection, they were ten separate battles. With reflection, you notice six came at night, after arguments. Three showed up on payday. Two arrived when you were bored and sitting in silence. Suddenly, the "random" urges aren't random at all, they're coded.

And once you see the code, you can prepare. Payday means pre-planning where the money goes. Arguments mean walking it out instead of stewing in resentment. Silence means adding a journal or a playlist so it doesn't swallow you.

Reflection turns chaos into a roadmap. Without it, cravings feel like ambushes. With it, they become forecasts.

Plain language:
You can't fight what you can't see. Reflection shines a flashlight on your cravings until they stop being surprises.

The Danger of Skipping Reflection

This is where many people slip: they think reflection is optional. They say, *"I'll just push forward. I don't need to look back."* But skipping reflection carries three big risks:

1. **You minimize your progress.** Without reflection, you forget the nights you said no, the mornings you woke up clean, the days you broke the loop. You only see failure, not growth.

2. **You exaggerate your failures.** One bad craving or slip feels like the whole truth because you're not weighing it against the dozens of times you succeeded.

3. **You miss the map.** Without reflection, you don't see the pattern. You keep calling cravings "random" when they're actually predictable.

This is why relapse often feels like it comes *"out of nowhere."* It didn't. The signs were there, you just didn't stop long enough to trace them.

Reflection is not indulgence. It's survival. It's what turns a craving from a weapon that blindsides you into a teacher that guides you.

Plain language:
If you don't stop and look, cravings will keep ambushing you. Reflection is how you stop fighting blind.

The Takeaway

Cravings are not monsters waiting to take you down. They are messengers, carrying information about your needs and stress points. Reflection is the practice that transforms cravings from chaos into a map. When you slow down, patterns emerge, progress becomes visible, and relapse loses its element of surprise.

The takeaway is this: cravings are not random attacks, they're coded signals. When you learn to read them, they stop being threats and start becoming guides.

Jordan's Hidden Pattern

Jordan was 35 and six months clean. He swore cravings came out of nowhere. "Sometimes I just get hit," he said. He'd be fine at work, then suddenly think about using on the way home.

His counselor gave him a challenge: track every craving for two weeks using a simple reflection map. At first, Jordan thought it was pointless. But slowly, a pattern emerged: every craving happened within an hour of finishing overtime.

He realized he was exhausted, hungry, and lonely after staying late at work. The substance had always been his shortcut to numbing that triple punch.

Once he saw the pattern, he changed the routine: he packed food, texted a friend before leaving, and committed to ten minutes of breathing before driving home. The cravings didn't vanish, but they lost their power. Because now, they weren't random attacks. They were predictable signals he knew how to meet.

That reflection saved him from relapse.

> "LISTEN, CRAVINGS ARE STUBBORN. THEY'LL SHOW UP WHETHER YOU INVITED THEM OR NOT. BUT HERE'S THE THING: THEY'RE NOT TRAPS. THEY'RE CLUES. EVERY TIME YOU MAP ONE, YOU STEAL A LITTLE BIT OF ITS POWER. DON'T RUN FROM THE URGE, STUDY IT. THE MORE YOU STUDY, THE LESS IT CAN SCARE YOU."
> UNCLE A

Tools & Exercises

Craving Reflection Map

Purpose: To track cravings and decode what they're really saying.
How to Do It:

1. When a craving hits, jot down:

   - Time of day
   - Situation (what was happening)
   - Mood (sad, anxious, lonely, bored, angry)
   - Thought ("I need it," "I can't do this," etc.)
   - Body sensation (tight chest, sweaty palms, restless legs)
   - What you did (response)
   - What you learned afterward

2. Repeat daily for two weeks. Look for patterns.
   Tip: Don't judge the craving. Treat it like data.

Trigger Timeline

Purpose: To see how cravings cluster in your daily or weekly rhythm.
Steps:

1. Draw a 24-hour clock or 7-day calendar.

2. Mark each time a craving hit this week.

3. At the end, review: are there hotspots? Late night? Payday? After arguments?

4. Write down one plan for each hotspot.

The Reframe Journal

Prompt: *"What did this craving teach me about myself today?"*
Steps:

1. Write down the craving.

2. Instead of asking, "Why did this happen?" ask, "What was it showing me?"

3. Identify one unmet need underneath the urge.

4. Write one action that could meet that need without using.

Weekly Reflection Circle (Group or Solo)

Purpose: To consolidate learning.

Steps:

1. At the end of the week, sit with your Craving Reflection Maps.

2. Highlight three repeated triggers.

3. Share them with a peer, counselor, or your journal.

4. Write: *"Next time this craving shows up, I'll…"*

Dr. Jones' Advisory	Nurse C's Note
In clinical terms, reflection is what transforms experience into learning. Without reflection, cravings remain raw, unprocessed stimuli that drive behavior. With reflection, they become coded patterns that can be predicted, interrupted, and reframed. For trauma survivors, this process is doubly important, it provides mastery where chaos once ruled. Encourage clients to treat reflection as non-negotiable, not optional.	Reflection is not just mental. It's neurological. Every time you stop and map a craving, you're training your prefrontal cortex, the decision-making center, to override the amygdala's fear response. You're literally rewiring your brain to see urges as signals instead of threats. That shift reduces anxiety and lowers relapse risk.

Reflection Prompt

- What's one craving this week that I thought was random?

- Looking back, what was it really connected to?

- How would I respond differently now that I see the pattern?

Closing Thought

Cravings will keep showing up. But they don't have to stay as enemies. Reflection turns them into teachers. Every urge you map, every pattern you uncover, every lesson you take away, it's all part of your survival guide.

Cravings aren't commands. They're reminders of where you've been, and signals pointing to where you need support next.

Chapter 10 – Identity Beyond the Craving

This Chapter Will Cover:

- Why identity must be spoken and claimed, not just silently held.

- How storytelling weaves cravings, shame, and victories into one integrated arc.

- Why recovery identity isn't about denying cravings, but anchoring yourself beyond them.

- Tools for crafting and speaking a Recovery Identity Statement.

CASEL Alignment:

- **Self-Awareness:** Recognizing that urges are experiences, not identity.

- **Self-Management:** Anchoring in self-statements and narrative practice.

- **Responsible Decision-Making:** Building resilience by consolidating identity beyond relapse fear.

Claiming Who You Are

Recovery doesn't end when the cravings stop. It deepens when you decide who you are in spite of them. Too many people define themselves by the battle: *"I'm someone who fights cravings every day."* But that definition keeps you orbiting around the urge, always tethered to the thing you don't want.

Here's the truth: you are more than what you fight. Identity in recovery has to go further than saying, *"I don't use."* It has to expand into: *"I live. I connect. I create. I love. I matter."*

Every craving you've walked through has given you proof. You endured the gray zone of silence. You faced the exhaustion that made mornings feel impossible. You mapped your loops, tracked your shame spirals, and built craving kits that kept you steady. These tools aren't just coping strategies; they are the receipts of who you are becoming. They show, in real time, that you are capable, resourceful, and resilient.

Plain language:
Your identity isn't your craving. Your identity is the person who survived it.

Why Speaking It Matters

Identity only solidifies when it's spoken. You can think about it all day long, but until you put words to it, it stays fragile and abstract. That's why recovery groups emphasize circles, sharing, and affirmations. Speaking aloud pulls the fragments together and gives them weight.

Think of it like this: cravings are loud. They shout in your head, repeating their scripts until you feel cornered. Reflection and tools quiet them down, but the echo lingers. Speaking your recovery identity out loud makes your truth louder than the craving.

This is why storytelling matters. It doesn't erase cravings, it reframes them. The urges become part of the narrative, not the headline. You don't pretend they never existed; you put them in their place: *chapters in your story, not the whole book.*

Plain language:
Until you tell your story, the craving is the headline. Once you tell it, the craving becomes a footnote.

When Identity Becomes the Anchor

Here's why this step is critical: cravings don't vanish forever. They will resurface, maybe not as often, maybe not as strong, but they'll come. The difference is that now, cravings no longer get to define you.

You've built your maps. You've practiced your resets. You've worked through shame spirals and anxiety static. You've learned reflection, built scaffolding, and tested your strength in silence. Now your anchor is identity: *I am more than my urge.*

Plain language:
Cravings fade, but identity remains.

The Takeaway

Cravings may still knock, but they don't get to hold the keys anymore. Recovery isn't just about resisting urges, it's about becoming someone whose life is bigger than the battle. When you speak your identity out loud, you plant it deeper than any craving can reach.

The takeaway is this: your recovery is not defined by what you avoid. It's defined by who you are becoming, steady, whole, and unshakably present.

Maria's Panic

Maria was nine months clean when she faced one of her hardest cravings yet. It didn't come from loneliness or shame, it came on a good day, right after she got a promotion. The joy felt overwhelming, and her brain whispered: *"You know how to make this feel even better."*

For a moment, she panicked. *Was she failing again?* But then she remembered her Recovery Identity Statement: *"I am someone who stays."* She spoke it out loud. She texted a peer, not to confess failure, but to claim strength. The craving still pulsed in her chest, but it passed.

The difference? Maria wasn't clinging to a tool in desperation. She wasn't bargaining with herself or shaming herself into compliance. She was standing in who she had already decided she was. Identity carried her when motivation wavered.

> "CRAVINGS ARE CHAPTERS, NOT TITLES. DON'T GIVE THEM THE POWER TO NAME YOUR WHOLE STORY. YOU DO THE NAMING. SAY IT OUT LOUD. WRITE IT DOWN. SHARE IT IN YOUR CIRCLE. EVERY TIME YOU CLAIM YOUR RECOVERY IDENTITY, YOU REMIND THE CRAVING IT DOESN'T GET THE LAST WORD." **UNCLE A**

Tools & Exercises

Recovery Identity Statement

Purpose: To create a personal anchor statement that solidifies recovery identity.
How to Do It:

1. Write one sentence that begins with *"I am…"* and defines you beyond cravings. Examples:

   - "I am someone who stays."

   - "I am present in my own life."

   - "I am building a family that doesn't fear me."

2. Keep it short enough to repeat in under 10 seconds.

3. Practice saying it out loud daily, especially when cravings whisper.

Reflection Letter

Prompt: *"This is who I am beyond the craving."*
Steps:

1. Write a one-page letter to yourself or a trusted peer.

2. Include three things you've learned about cravings, three tools you've mastered, and three truths about who you are now.

3. Read it aloud to yourself at least once. Speaking it is what seals it.

Story Circle Integration

Purpose: To share your recovery identity safely in community.
Steps:

1. Gather with a group, or with one trusted person.

2. Each person shares one craving story but framed through the lens of victory or growth.

3. After sharing, the group responds with affirmation, not advice. Example: "We see your strength."

Group Affirmation Ritual

Purpose: To root identity in community validation.
Steps:

1. After each story, the group repeats together:

   - "We see your strength."

   - "We see your growth."

   - "We believe in your next step."

2. Write the affirmation in your journal afterward as a reminder.

Dr. Jones' Advisory	Nurse C's Note
Clinically, this is consolidation. Recovery requires integration, not just of tools, but of self. When clients create and claim identity statements, they are practicing narrative repair. They move from being defined by trauma and cravings to being defined by growth and resilience. This is long-term relapse prevention.	When you speak your recovery identity aloud, your body responds. The vagus nerve calms, cortisol lowers, and dopamine pathways begin to link identity with safety instead of survival. This is why spoken identity matters; it doesn't just change your mind. It changes your nervous system.

Reflection Prompt

- What words do I want to define me beyond cravings?

- How would I describe my recovery identity in one sentence?

- Who can I share it with this week to anchor it deeper?

Closing Thought

Cravings will still come. But they don't command your story anymore. Your identity does. Every time you write it, speak it, and live it, you reinforce a truth cravings can't erase:

You are not your urge. You are your recovery.

"Cravings don't drive your life. You do."

You're Not Broken - You're Becoming

This Was Never Just About Cravings

Let's be real.

If cravings were just about wanting something, a single "no" would fix it. But they're not. Cravings are about *needing* something. Safety. Numbness. Power. Connection. Escape. Identity.

You didn't just want to use. You wanted *relief*. And in a body that had no map for comfort, the craving showed up like a rescue.

This book wasn't just about saying no. It was about understanding why the yes always made sense in the moment.

And more importantly, about building a life where the yes doesn't have to be your only option.

You Interrupted the Spiral

By now, you've:

- Mapped out your craving loops
- Named the lies your brain whispers
- Learned what green, yellow, and red feel like
- Surfed urges without drowning
- Practiced narrating the craving out loud
- Identified where anxiety and shame sneak in

But more than any of that?

You've stayed. You've sat in the heat instead of burning it all down.

That's *recovery*.

Not perfection. Not abstinence as identity.

But presence. Pattern-breaking. Power reclaimed one pause at a time.

What Comes Next

You might still get cravings. Let's not lie about that.

But now, they're not mysteries.

Now, you've got a map.

Keep your tools close:

- Your **STOPLIGHT Card** isn't just paper — it's your boundary line.
- Your **Craving Log** is a record of proof: You don't respond the way you used to.
- Your **Urge Surf Scripts**? They've made space where panic used to live.

And keep noticing:

- What lies keep coming back?
- What state makes you most vulnerable?
- Who helps you pause — and who pushes you back into the loop?

This isn't over. But neither are you.

YOU MADE IT THROUGH THE STORM, AND MAYBE YOU'RE SOAKED, MAYBE YOU'RE SHAKING, BUT YOU'RE STILL UPRIGHT. AND YOU'RE LEARNING TO WALK DIFFERENTLY NOW.

THE OLD PATH - THE ONE THAT STARTED WITH STRESS AND ENDED WITH SHAME, DOESN'T OWN YOU ANYMORE.

YOU HAVE CHOICES NOW. YOU KNOW YOUR CRAVING PATTERN. YOU'VE LEARNED TO SPEAK THE CRAVING LIE OUT LOUD, TO CALL IT WHAT IT IS. AND THAT'S NO SMALL THING.

YOU'RE NOT BROKEN.
YOU'RE BECOMING.
UNCLE A

Dr. Jones' Advisory	Nurse C's Note
If you're reading this and still struggling with self-trust, here's what I'll say: You do not need to be perfectly regulated to be in recovery. You need curiosity. Self-awareness. A willingness to pause and check in. That's what builds emotional resilience. That's what turns recovery from a punishment into a process of becoming whole.	Your body remembers the high and the crash, and everything in between. It also remembers safety, even if it hasn't felt it in years. Keep hydrating. Keep eating real food. Keep sleeping when you can. And don't ignore your body's signals. Tiredness, tension, and tightness aren't weaknesses. They're messages. Listen. You don't just heal with therapy. You heal with rest, rhythm, and nourishment.

FINAL Reflection: Keep Asking

- What lies still feel believable?
- What craving do I miss the most - and what need was it meeting?
- How does it feel to know I have the power to pause?

Write. Don't just think it. Keep this page close.